BUILDING
furniture FOR
COUNTRY LIVING

edited by
JIM STACK

POPULAR WOODWORKING BOOKS
CINCINNATI, OHIO
www.popularwoodworking.com

read this important safety notice

To prevent accidents, keep safety in mind while you work. Use the safety guards installed on power equipment; they are for your protection. When working on power equipment, keep fingers away from saw blades, wear safety goggles to prevent injuries from flying wood chips and sawdust, wear hearing protection and consider installing a dust vacuum to reduce the amount of airborne sawdust in your woodshop. Don't wear loose clothing, such as neckties or shirts with loose sleeves, or jewelry, such as rings, necklaces or bracelets, when working on power equipment. Tie back long hair to prevent it from getting caught in your equipment. People who are sensitive to certain chemicals should check the chemical content of any product before using it. Glass shelving should have all edges polished and must be tempered. Untempered glass shelves may shatter and can cause serious bodily injury. Tempered shelves are very strong and if they break will just crumble, minimizing personal injury. The authors and editors who compiled this book have tried to make the contents as accurate and correct as possible. Plans, illustrations, photographs and text have been carefully checked. All instructions, plans and projects should be carefully read, studied and understood before beginning construction. Due to the variability of local conditions, construction materials, skill levels, etc., neither the author nor Popular Woodworking Books assumes any responsibility for any accidents, injuries, damages or other losses incurred resulting from the material presented in this book. Prices listed for supplies and equipment were current at the time of publication and are subject to change.

metric conversion chart

to convert	to	multiply by
Inches	Centimeters	2.54
Centimeters	Inches	0.4
Feet	Centimeters	30.5
Centimeters	Feet	0.03
Yards	Meters	0.9
Meters	Yards	1.1

Building Furniture for Country Living. Copyright © 2007 by Popular Woodworking Books. Printed and bound in China. All rights reserved. No part of this book may be reproduced in any form or by any electronic or mechanical means including information storage and retrieval systems without permission in writing from the publisher, except by a reviewer, who may quote brief passages in a review. Published by Popular Woodworking Books, an imprint of F+W Publications, Inc., 4700 East Galbraith Road, Cincinnati, Ohio, 45236. First edition.

Distributed in Canada by Fraser Direct
100 Armstrong Avenue
Georgetown, Ontario L7G 5S4
Canada

Distributed in the U.K. and Europe by David & Charles
Brunel House
Newton Abbot
Devon TQ12 4PU
England
Tel: (+44) 1626 323200
Fax: (+44) 1626 323319
E-mail: postmaster@davidandcharles.co.uk

Distributed in Australia by Capricorn Link
P.O. Box 704
Windsor, NSW 2756
Australia

Visit our Web site at www.popularwoodworking.com for information on more resources for woodworkers.

Other fine Popular Woodworking Books are available from your local bookstore or direct from the publisher.

11   10   09   08   07   5   4   3   2   1

Library of Congress Cataloging-in-Publication Data

Building furniture for country living / edited by Jim Stack. -- 1st ed.
     p. cm.
   Includes index.
   ISBN-13: 978-1-55870-788-7 (pbk. : alk. paper)
   ISBN-10: 1-55870-788-3 (pbk. : alk. paper)
   1. Furniture making. 2. Country furniture. I. Stack, Jim, 1951- II. Popular woodworking.
   TT194.B837 2007
   684.1--dc22
                              2006037227

Acquisitions editor: David Thiel
Editor: Jim Stack
Cover design: Brian Roeth
Interior design: Amy Wilkin, Dragonfly Graphics, L.L.C.
Production coordinator: Jennifer Wagner
Photographers: Al Parrish (project openers), Jim Stack, Dave Griessmann
Illustrators: Melanie Powell, Kevin Pierce

F+W PUBLICATIONS, INC.

about the authors

Thane Lorbach repairs and restores antique furniture and builds new furniture. He is working towards owning his own furniture making business. Thane lives in Cincinnati, Ohio

Dave Griessman builds reproduction furniture in his "free" time and is working towards owning his own furniture making business. Dave lives in Cincinnati, Ohio.

Kerry Pierce is a retired high school English teacher who has built Shaker chairs for over 20 years and is a contributing author for *Woodcraft* and *Woodworks* magazines. He is also the author of several woodworking books including, *Quick & Easy Jigs & Fixtures*, *The Wood Stash Project Book*, *The Used Lumber Project Book*, *Authentic Shaker Furniture* and *Pleasant Hill Shaker Furniture*. Kerry lives in Lancaster, Ohio.

Andy McCormick is a cabinetmaker and furniture maker who runs his own shop in Liberty, Indiana.

Glen Huey is a Senior Editor for *Popular Woodworking* magazine. He has built and still builds reproduction furniture and is the author of *Fine Furniture for a Lifetime*, *Building Fine Furniture* and *Glen Huey's Guide to Building Period Furniture*, all published by *Popular Woodworking Books*. Glen lives in Middletown, Ohio.

Bill Hylton is a longtime woodworker and woodworking writer. He is a frequent contributor to *The Woodworker's Journal* and has written many woodworking books, including *Rodale's Illustrated Cabinetmaking*, *Router Magic*, *Country Pine*, *Woodworking with the Router* (with Fred Matlack), *Handcrafted Shelves & Cabinets* (with Amy Rowland), *Chests of Drawers* and *Bill Hylton's Power-Tool Joinery*. Bill lives in Kempton, Pennsylvania.

Jim Stack is Senior Editor for *Popular Woodworking Books*. He worked in commericial cabinetmaking and furniture making shops for over 20 years. He is the author of *Northwoods Furniture*, *The Biscuit Joiner Project Book*, *Design Your Own Furniture*, *Building the Perfect Tool Chest*, *Cutting-Edge Router Projects* and most recently *Box by Box*. All books are published by *Popular Woodworking Books*.

acknowledgements

I'd like to thank **the builders** of the furniture pieces presented in this book. They were easy to work with and took pride in their finished projects, as well they should.

Amy Wilkin designed this book and, in my opinion, did a great job of giving a country feel to the book by using earth-tone colors. She also had the tricky task of taking my crude layout of all the materials and putting them into the visual treat you now hold in your hands.

Jennifer Wagner is responsible for making sure all the book materials make it intact to the printer so the book gets to see the light of day. She once again did this and made it look easy.

Al Parrish is a photographer who manipulates and paints with light. The chapter opener photos are, by themselves, works of art that serve (we hope!) to inspire you to want to build these projects for your own enjoyment and the enjoyment of others.

The Cincinnati, Ohio area has a lot of great woodworkers and I wanted to let some of them demonstrate and teach how they build furniture.

There are several ways to do things and get the same results. For example, Glen Huey and Dave Griessmann cut their mortise-and-tenon joinery the same way. Bill Hylton (who lives out of the Cincinnati area but nonetheless has country-furniture roots) cuts his mortise-and-tenon joinery differently. And I cut mine using yet another method. The results are all the same in that we end up with a frame that looks great and will be strong for generations.

I chose the furniture projects for this book based upon my own memory of pieces I've seen in farmhouses and homes I've visited over the years.

The 2-drawer valet is based on an oak 2-drawer dresser and a smaller cabinet (it was originally designed to store hats). The fronts of the drawers and the door on the cabinet had relief carvings. The 3-drawer dresser with 2 small drawer boxes on top was designed based on an oak piece that has been in my mother's family for generations.

The lamp table is based on an oak table with bead-turned splayed legs and a square top with scroll-shaped edges and a fixed shelf set into all four legs.

The steps are based on Shaker-style step stools.

The wastebasket was inspired by a round Arts-and-Crafts wastebasket made of wooden slats attached to 2 iron rings.

The dining table is an interpretation of a harvest table, as is the drop-leaf kitchen table.

The drop-front secretary is a plain version of dozens of configurations of this drop-front desk style.

To make any of the projects requires intermediate to advanced woodworking skills. For example, the seemingly simple wastebasket is an exercise in building tapered frame-and-panel sides and cutting compound angles.

The woods of choice for country-style furniture are typically white pine or oak. We've shown that cherry, white oak, maple and poplar are also good choices.

We hope you are inspired to build these (or similar) pieces of furniture to add that country feel to your own homes.

stepstool

A stepstool is a necessity in every home. Most aren't very attractive. Until I built this design, mine was always hidden in a closet. At my house, this piece functions as both a stepstool and a place for my kids to sit. It is, in fact, a piece of furniture. You can build this project in a weekend or less and it's not difficult to do. If you want to build a piece of furniture but need to hone your woodworking skills, this is a great project to take on.

The construction is straightforward, and you can complete the entire piece using basic tools. Buy your wood already surfaced (flat and square) and the main power tools you will need are a table saw, jigsaw or band saw, and a drill. In the course of this project you will make matching risers, learn a fun way to draw a curve and use dowels to hide screws and lend a decorative look to your work. So, step right up...

by Thane Lorbach

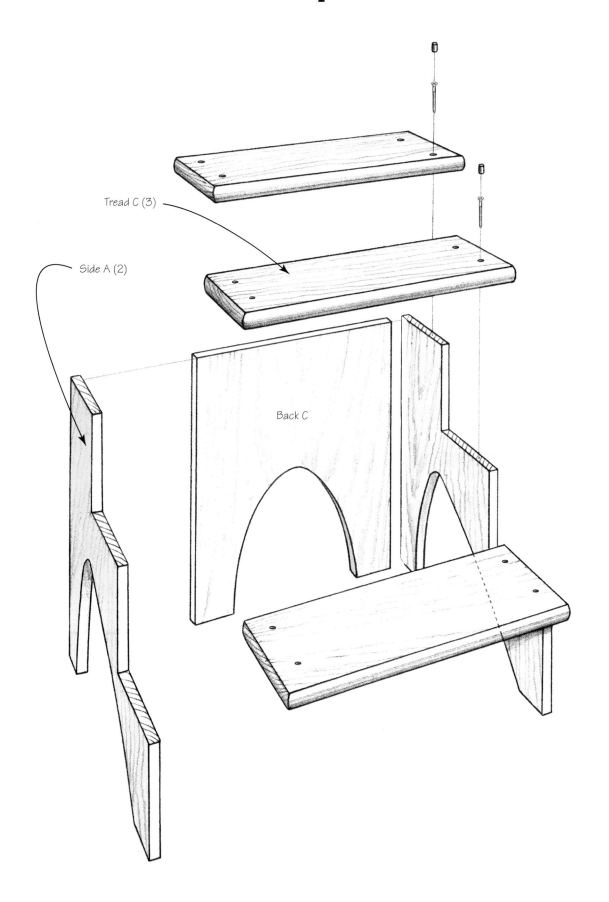

Tread C (3)

Side A (2)

Back C

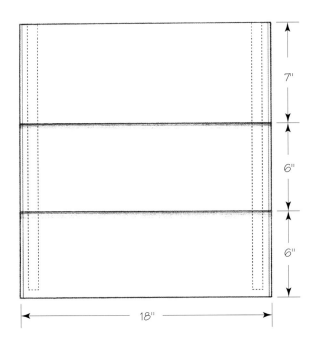

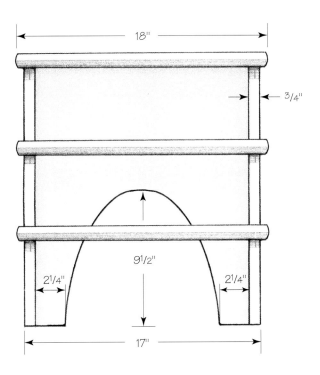

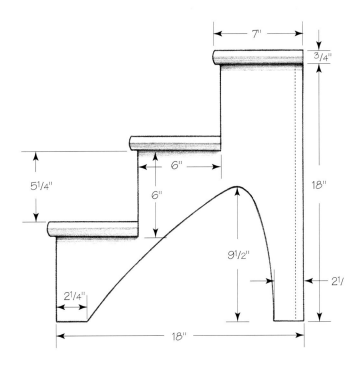

REFERENCE	QUANTITY	PART	STOCK	THICKNESS		WIDTH		LENGTH		COMMENTS
A	2	sides	white oak	¾	(19)	18	(457)	18	(457)	
B	1	back	white oak	¾	(19)	15½	(394)	18	(457)	
C	3	treads	white oak	¾	(19)	7	(178)	18	(457)	

hardware & supplies

- 24—No. 8 × 2" (50mm) flathead wood screws
- wood glue
- stain
- polyurethane finish

1 After purchasing or milling all of the stock, rip all parts to width. To make the back, edge glue as many pieces of wood as needed to achieve the final width.

2 Square up one end of each board and mark that end using a pencil.

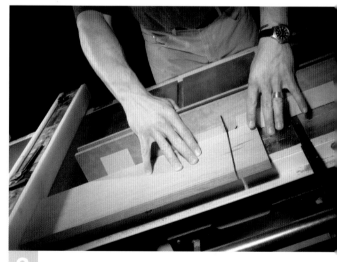

3 The sides are made of three boards glued together to create the notches for the steps. Reference the squared end of the side boards against the fence. Cut the two longest side boards and the back boards to length. Move the saw fence and cut the middle side boards. Set the fence again and cut the shortest side pieces.

4 I found it easiest to glue up the sides two boards at a time using a spacer cut to step height.

5 Glue the short sideboard in place to complete the side assembly. (The bottom board square, so make sure the grain runs vertically.)

6 To visually lighten the stepstool and to add some personal creativity to the project, I cut curves in the back and both sides. After gluing the boards together to make the back, lay the back on a piece of cardboard a couple inches from the bottom edge and draw a line around the perimeter. Determine how tall and wide you want your curve to be. Place a sacrificial board (plywood or medium density fiberboard [MDF]) under the cardboard and drive a nail at the curve's tallest point in the center (left to right) of the back. Drive nails on the bottom line at the curve's widest point, one on each side. Tie a string onto the bottom left nail, bring it over the top nail and loop it twice around the bottom right nail. Place a pencil inside the string and draw the curve. Loosen or tighten the string to form the curve you want. The looser you have the string, the wider and rounder your curve will be. For the curves in the sides, follow the same procedure, but offset the top nail instead of centering it. Once you have your desired curves drawn on cardboard, cut them out with a utility knife and use them to draw the curves onto the back and sides of your project. Using a jigsaw or band saw, cut out the curves in both sides and the back. Then use a file and sandpaper, or a spindle sander, to clean up the saw marks.

7 Lay the sides back edge to back edge. Mark the screw hole locations for attaching the sides to the back.

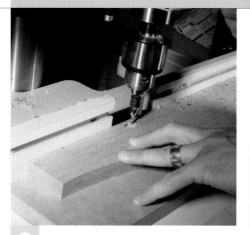

9 Sand the inside of the back. Then clamp the back and sides together and install the screws. You can use glue in addition to screws but it's not necessary.

8 Because the back is ³⁄₄" (19mm) thick, drill the holes ³⁄₈" (9mm) from the back edge of each side using a countersink bit. Drill the holes so the countersink bit creates a ¹⁄₄" (16mm)-deep hole that will accept a plug to hide the screw head.

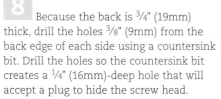

10 Using part of a roundover router bit, ease the front edges and ends of the treads. Rout the end-grain first, taking a very light pass. Routing the long-grain after routing both ends cleans up any tear-out caused by routing the end-grain. Mark the back edges of the treads so you don't accidentally roundover the back edges. A file, rasp, sandpaper or block plane can also be used to create the roundover on the treads.

11 After sanding the entire piece (sides, back and treads), attach the treads to the base assembly using screws and wood plugs. Cut a scrap piece of wood the same width as the back and place it between the two sides at the bottom step so the sides will remain parallel. Start with the bottom tread. For a more dramatic look, choose a contrasting wood for the plugs.

My kitchen has a white oak floor with a natural finish so I chose not to stain this piece. Since this piece will get a lot of wear, I applied four coats of polyurethane, rubbing with No.0000 steel wool between each coat — including the final coat — for a nice semigloss look.

Applying stain and polyurethane can change the wood's color and appearance, so use some scrap wood from your project as a test piece. Experiment with different stains and finishes.

wastebasket

A simple wastebasket — not so fast! This piece is more complicated than it looks. Building this wastebasket teaches you about tapered frames and panels, how to cut parallel and opposite angles, how to resaw and bookmatch. In addition, you'll learn a simple mortise-and-tenon technique and a fast and simple way to cut miters on a jointer.

More reasons to love this project: It's small so it doesn't require a great deal of wood and requires no hardware. It's also beautiful, a little challenging and makes a great finishing touch for a home office.

by Thane Lorbach

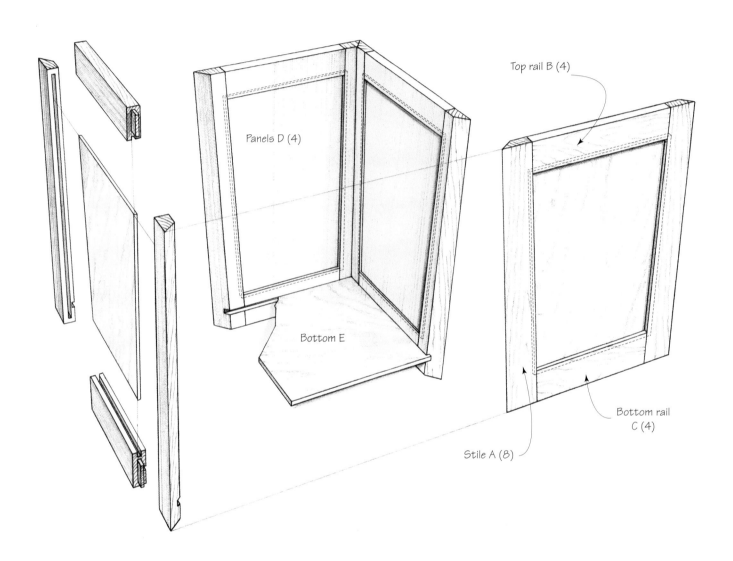

Top rail B (4)

Panels D (4)

Bottom E

Bottom rail C (4)

Stile A (8)

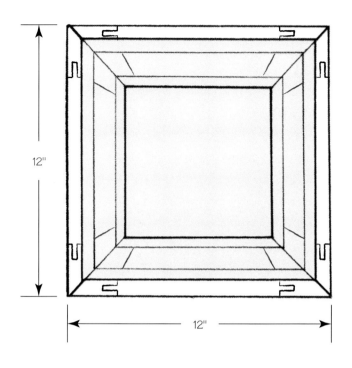

12"

12"

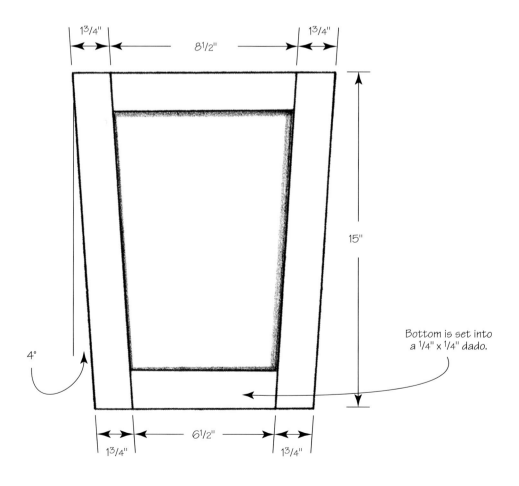

1³/₄"

8¹/₂"

1³/₄"

15"

4°

6¹/₂"

1³/₄"

1³/₄"

Bottom is set into
a ¹/₄" x ¹/₄" dado.

CUTTING LIST ■ *wastebasket* inches (millimeters)

REFERENCE	QUANTITY	PART	STOCK	THICKNESS		WIDTH		LENGTH		COMMENTS
A	8	stiles	white oak	¾	(19)	1¾	(44)	15³⁄₁₆	(386)	angled cut both ends
B	4	top rails	white oak	¾	(19)	1¾	(44)	9½	(241)	½" (13mm) tenons both ends
C	4	bottom rails	white oak	¾	(19)	1¾	(45)	7¾	(197)	
D	4	panels	white oak	¼	(6)	9	(229)	11½	(292)	
E	1	bottom	white oak	¼	(6)	9¼	(235)	9¼	(235)	

hardware & supplies

- wood glue
- stain
- polyurethane finish

1 Set the miter gauge to 4° and make a cut on one end of all of the rails and stiles.

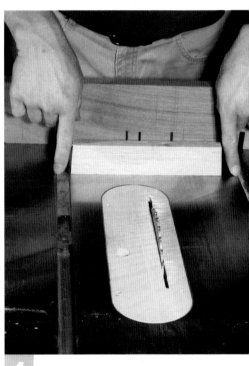

2 Leave the miter gauge at the same setting and set the fence to the stile length, then flip the stile over end for end, reference the cut end flat against the fence and make the second cut. This will make the two parallel cuts. When one end of a stile is placed flat on the table, the stile will stand at a 4° angle. Cut all eight stiles to length.

3 Set the fence for the length of the bottom rails. (Don't forget to add the length of both tenons before cutting the rails to length.) Flip the rail end for end (but not over). Note that the cut end will not sit flush against the fence, only the tip will touch the fence. Make the second cut on the four bottom rails. Reset fence to the length of the top rails and make the cuts.

4 The rails will have opposite angles and the stiles will have parallel angles. I'm showing exaggerated opposite angles on the rails using my fingers.

5 Mark the center of one of the rails. Using a square tooth blade, position the fence so the blade will cut to one side of the centerline. Raise the blade to ½" (13mm) high and cut a through groove in one edge of all of the rails and stiles. For the stiles, choose either edge for your groove. For the longer top rail, make the groove in the tapered, shorter edge. For the shorter bottom rail make the groove in the wider edge. This can get confusing, so mark the edges to be grooved.

6 To assure the groove is centered, make the first cut, then turn the rails and stiles 180°, referencing the other side against the fence and make the second cut. This centers the groove in the parts to accept the floating side panel. Make fence adjustments if necessary so the groove is ¼" (6mm)-wide. After your final pass leave the blade at the same height in order to cut your tenons.

7 I find it helpful to use a shop-made push block when cutting the tenons. This allows you to clamp the rails to the push block at the appropriate angle. If you don't use a push block or a tenon cutting jig here, the piece could move during a cut—and that can be dangerous. The push block is shown on its side. For the tenons, it is used standing upright with the small block on top.

8 Cut the tenons by clamping the rail to the push block with the cut end on the rail resting flat on the saw's table. Set the fence so the blade will cut the outer part of the tenon.

9 Turn the rail 180°, making sure the end is flat on the table saw (it will angle the opposite direction), and cut the other side of the tenon. Repeat these two cuts on both ends of all eight rails before moving your fence.

10 Move the table saw fence slightly toward the blade and make another pass. Turn the rail and make the second pass. Cut both ends of all eight rails at this setting before moving your fence. Continue this process, easing the fence in just slightly, until the tenons fit snugly into the grooves in the stiles. Remember, the distance the fence is moved is double the amount of material being removed. Make small adjustments.

11 Because you used the same blade height when cutting the grooves for the floating panels and the tenons, the tenons will be the correct length to fit perfectly in the groove. (The grooves for the floating panels also serve as the mortises.)

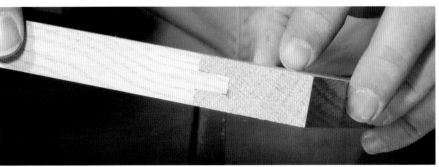

12 The tops of the stiles will be visable when the wastebasket is finished. Fit the end of the tenons so they bottom out in the grooves. It's not necessary to leave a space for glue.

13 I chose to resaw and bookmatch the quartersawn white oak to make the floating panels. (This technique requires you to slice a board in half, opening the two pieces like a book. When glued together, one piece is a mirror image of the other.) The graining in the bookmatched panels for this particular piece looks very similar to the stems of a large leaf. You can also make the panel wiht multiple hardwood boards glued together or a piece of ¼" (6mm)-thick plywood. If you choose to use plywood, find a piece that is veneered on both sides because both sides will be visible.

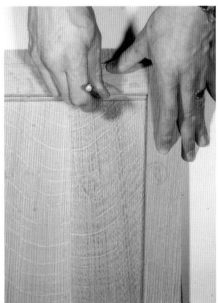

15 I used a piece of scrap that was just under ½" (13mm) thick to trace the final size for the panel. The panel shouldn't bottom out in the grooves. Keep the width slightly narrower, which allows the panel to "float" inside the grooves. This will allow the board to expand and contract over the seasons with little risk of warping or cracking.

14 Place a dry-fitted frame on top of each panel and trace a line around the inside of the frame.

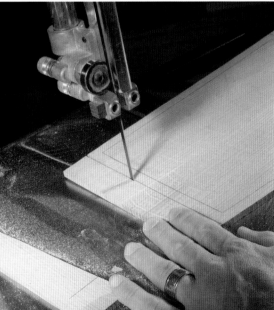

16 Cut all the panels to size by cutting on the *outside* line. It might be helpful to erase or sand off the inside line so you don't cut on the wrong one.

17 If you don't have access to a jointer, it's easier to cut the long miters on the stiles before gluing everything together. Set the table saw blade at 45° and set the fence so the blade will take only enough stock to allow the edge to come to a point. These edges are fragile, so pad the edges during glue up and use very little clamping pressure to avoid damaging the edges.

18 If you have access to a jointer, after gluing up the frames, set the jointer fence to 45° and set the infeed table so it takes no more than a $1/16$" (2mm)-deep cut. Make as many passes as necessary to complete the miter (until the face and edge meet at a point). While making the miter, count the number of passes you make on the jointer and cut the remaining miters, making this same number of passes for each one.

19 Set the table saw blade angle at 4° and cut the dado to accept the bottom. It is important to cut the long miters before cutting this dado. Otherwise, the jointer could cause the small piece of wood at the bottom of the dado to splinter off.

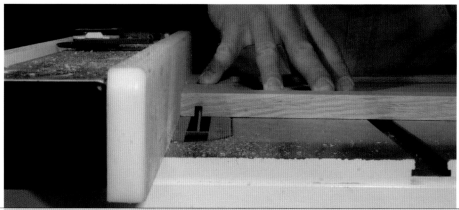

20 Move the saw's fence and cut the dado to final width.

21 Using the same 4° blade angle, cut the bevel on the top edge of the frame assemblies. This bevel will allow the completed wastebasket to sit flat on the floor. When cutting the top angle, the inside of the panel faces up (for a left-tilting saw) or down (for a right tilting saw).

22 Reset the fence to cut the bevel for the bottom edge. The top and bottom bevel cuts should be parallel to each other.

23 Dry fit the frames together and measure for the bottom. After cutting the bottom to fit, lay all four frames on a flat surface with the outsides facing up. Butt the sharp edges of the miters together and tape the three joints.

24 Use a brush to spread glue on all of the miters. To keep the bottom from moving and rattling, put a dab of glue in the center of two opposite bottom dadoes.

25 Insert the bottom, fold the parts together and tape the final joint. I chose to use an oil stain on this wastebasket. Use scrap to try different colors until you come up with one you like. I created my color by mixing five parts red mahogany and one part dark walnut oil-based stains. I applied three coats of wipe-on polyurethane since this piece will be treated like "trash."

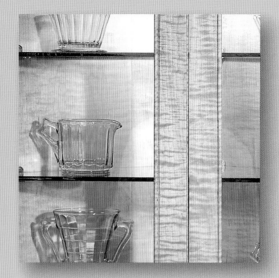

corner
wall cabinet

The design antecedents of this little corner cupboard are difficult to identify. The corner cabinet form has a long history in the genre of American country furniture and some of the details — the band sawn profile at the bottom of the cabinet, for example, suggest early antecedents. However, the mouldings were cut with late 19th-century planes and the scallops below the doors were borrowed from a late 19th-century source. So, although it is clearly a piece that has historical roots, those roots reach out in several directions.

No matter what its history, I like the way it looks.

by Kerry Pierce

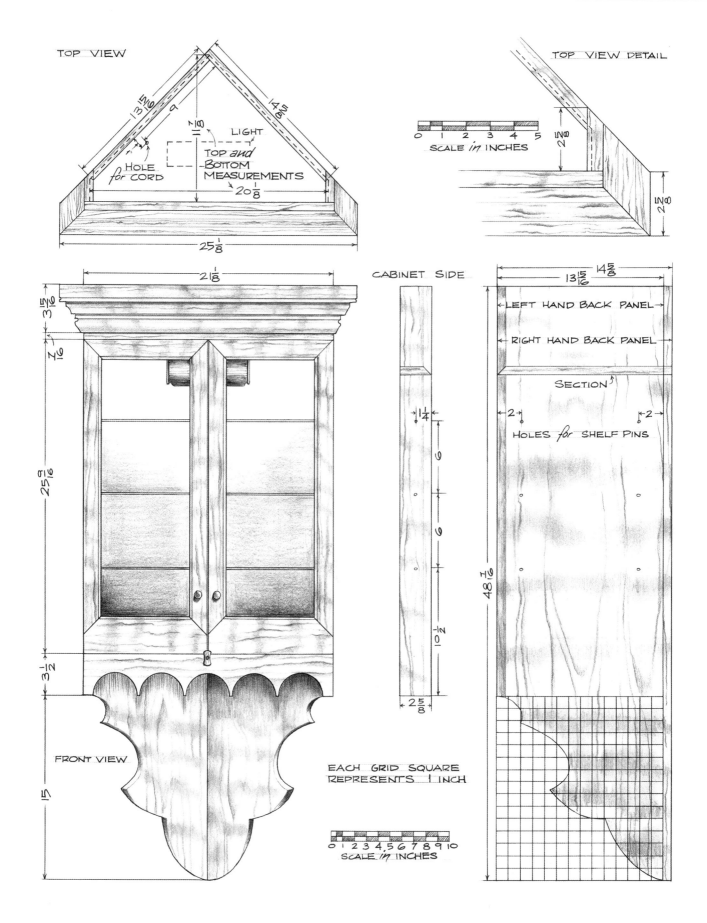

TOP VIEW

$13\frac{15}{16}$

9

$14\frac{5}{8}$

$1\frac{7}{8}$

LIGHT

Hole for CORD

TOP *and* BOTTOM MEASUREMENTS

$20\frac{1}{8}$

$25\frac{1}{8}$

TOP VIEW DETAIL

0 1 2 3 4 5

SCALE *in* INCHES

$2\frac{5}{8}$

$2\frac{5}{8}$

$21\frac{1}{8}$

$3\frac{15}{16}$

$2\frac{7}{16}$

$25\frac{9}{16}$

$3\frac{1}{2}$

15

FRONT VIEW

CABINET SIDE

$1\frac{1}{4}$

6

6

$10\frac{1}{2}$

$2\frac{5}{8}$

EACH GRID SQUARE REPRESENTS 1 INCH

0 1 2 3 4 5 6 7 8 9 10

SCALE *in* INCHES

$13\frac{15}{16}$

$14\frac{5}{8}$

LEFT HAND BACK PANEL

RIGHT HAND BACK PANEL

SECTION

2

2

HOLES *for* SHELF PINS

$48\frac{1}{16}$

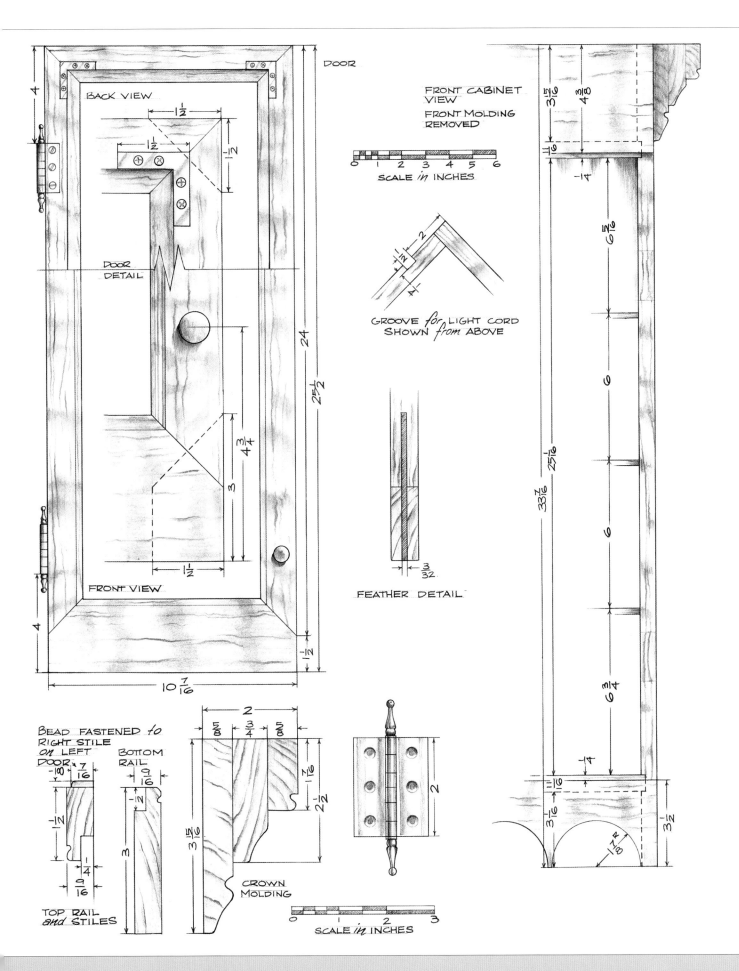

DOOR

BACK VIEW

1½

1½

1½

24

25½

DOOR DETAIL

4¾

3

1½

FRONT VIEW

4

4

1½

10 7⁄16

FRONT CABINET VIEW

FRONT MOLDING REMOVED

0 1 2 3 4 5 6
SCALE in INCHES

2

½

¼

GROOVE for LIGHT CORD SHOWN from ABOVE

3⁄32

FEATHER DETAIL

3 5⁄16

4 3⁄8

1⁄16

¼

6 5⁄16

6

33 7⁄16

25 1⁄16

6

6¾

¼

1⁄16

3 1⁄16

3½

R 7⁄8

BEAD FASTENED to RIGHT STILE on LEFT DOOR

7⁄16

10⁄10

1½

¼

9⁄16

BOTTOM RAIL

9⁄16

½

3

TOP RAIL and STILES

2

5⁄16

¾

5⁄16

7⁄16

2½

3 5⁄16

CROWN MOLDING

2

0 1 2 3
SCALE in INCHES

CUTTING LIST ■ *corner wall cabinet* inches (millimeters)

REFERENCE	QUANTITY	PART	STOCK	THICKNESS		WIDTH		LENGTH		COMMENTS
A	1	right back panel	maple	$^{11}/_{16}$	(17)	$14^5/_8$	(371)	$48^7/_{16}$	(1230)	
B	1	left back panel	maple	$^{11}/_{16}$	(17)	$13^{15}/_{16}$	(354)	$48^7/_{16}$	(1230)	
C	1	right cabinet side	maple	$^{11}/_{16}$	(17)	$2^5/_8$	(67)	$33^7/_{16}$	(849)	
D	1	left cabinet side	maple	$^{11}/_{16}$	(17)	$2^5/_8$	(67)	$33^7/_{16}$	(849)	
E	2	top and bottom	maple	$^{11}/_{16}$	(17)	$11^7/_8$	(302)	$20^1/_8$	(511)	
F	1	filler strip under crown	maple	$^{11}/_{16}$	(17)	$4^3/_8$	(111)	$21^1/_8$	(536)	
G	1	face below doors	maple	$^{11}/_{16}$	(17)	$3^1/_2$	(89)	$21^1/_8$	(536)	
H	1	top crown moulding	maple	$^5/_8$	(16)	$3^1/_8$	(79)	40	(102)	
J	1	middle crown moulding	maple	$^3/_4$	(19)	$4^3/_8$	(111)	40	(102)	
K	1	bottom crown moulding	maple	$^5/_8$	(16)	$3^{15}/_{16}$	(100)	40	(102)	after gluing moulding parts together, cut to needed lengths
L	4	door stiles	maple	$^9/_{16}$	(14)	$1^1/_2$	(38)	24	(610)	
M	2	door top rails	maple	$^9/_{16}$	(14)	$1^1/_2$	(38)	$10^7/_{16}$	(265)	
N	2	door bottom rails	maple	$^9/_{16}$	(14)	3	(76)	$10^7/_{16}$	(265)	
P	8	splines	maple	1	(25)	7	(178)	$32^3/_8$	(822)	
Q	2	arm supports	maple	$^3/_{32}$	(2)	$1^1/_2$	(38)	$1^1/_2$	(38)	cut to fit

hardware & supplies

- 20—No. 8 × 1$^5/_8$" (40mm) drywall or carcase screws
- 12—No. 8 × 2" (50mm) drywall or carcase screws
- 2—$^5/_8$" (16mm) × 5" (130mm) lag bolts
- 3—tempered glass shelves $^1/_2$" (6mm) × 1$^{15}/_{16}$" (287mm) × 19$^1/_2$" (495mm)
- 4—brass decorator hinges Woodcraft No.16R47
- 1 bag—brass bracket-style shelf supports Woodcraft No. 27114
- 2—brass knobs
- 1—curio cabinet light

1 Glue up the panels for the cabinet's two back sections, making sure they remain flat under clamping pressure.

2 After panels have been planed to flatness, rip them to width (be sure the outside edge of each panel is ripped at a 45° angle) and cut them to length. Using a cutoff box like the one I'm using will help you make accurate crosscuts on wide panels.

3 After you've cut the profile at the bottom of the two back panels with a saber saw and ripped out and cut to length the two very narrow side panels (don't forget the 45° angle along one edge), take a few moments to do some careful layout of the locations of the dadoes. This is another of those very important first steps.

4 When the layout work has been completed, you're ready to cut the dadoes into which the cabinet top and bottom will be fastened. These can be cut on a table saw with a dado cutter or with a router equipped with a straight bit. They can also be cut with a dado plane, as shown here. If you're using a dado plane, clamp a batten adjacent to the planned dado. Then run the plane along the batten until the plane's depth stop bottoms out.

5 Before you fasten anything together, lay out the cabinet's four major pieces and study them to be sure everything will come together properly. Because of its unusual geometry, a corner cabinet presents some assembly challenges which are best solved by stopping from time to time to study the work in progress. Notice that all four of these components have been ripped with one edge at a 45° angle.

6 In order to align the cabinet's two back panels so that I could screw them together, I tightened one panel edge-up in my side vise and created a support for the lapping panel using a footstool and a couple of pieces of scrap material. I then turned in a line of 2" (50mm) drywall screws. The array of drills is necessary for the different kinds of holes you need to drill at each location. The drill on the left is equipped with a countersink bit for the screw head. The two drills adjacent to that are fit with standard bits—one for the through hole in the lapping panel, the other for the threaded hole in the bottom panel.

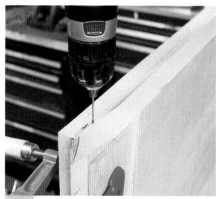

8 I fitted a ¼" (6mm) plywood pattern before I cut out the top and bottom. (I later cut this pattern to the correct size for the three glass shelves and dropped it off at the glass shop.) I then screwed the top and bottom into their dadoes.

7 Before I could fasten the narrow cabinet sides to the back panels, I first created a kind of cradle for them by clamping a batten on the back of the cabinet back. The narrow cabinet side then slipped into the 45° slot. I tapped a few finish nails into some predrilled holes in the cabinet sides. I didn't intend for the finish nails to hold the cabinet sides permanently in place, only until I could screw them to the cabinet top and bottom and then glue two front pieces in place. The set-and-filled nail holes are a bit unsightly, but when the job is finished, they'll be tucked up tight against the wall.

9 The front of the cabinet is flush with the doors so I added a filler strip at the top of the cabinet (visible under the crown moulding), as well as the scroll below the doors. Each of these pieces is the same thickness as the doors and each is held in place with glue. Cut the miters for your mouldings on your table saw.

moulding-making options

I have always made use of hand planes—to fine tune a tenon, to dress a panel too wide for my planer, to smooth a patch on a partially completed piece of casework—but since a bout of lymphoma, I have shifted from doing perhaps 20 to 25 percent of my shaping and smoothing with hand planes to doing 85 to 90 percent of this work with hand planes.

I set out on this new approach for reasons of health, but the switch from machine tools to hand tools has been beneficial in ways wholly unconnected to my health, introducing me to new and, in many instances, better ways of working.

Sticking mouldings in hard, figured maple with hand planes is hard work. (On the days I stuck mouldings, I passed on my afternoon walk.) But smoothing panels with a well-tuned infill plane is woodworking at its very best: rhythmic, soothing, satisfying and quiet. That's the most important thing. It's possible to think when you're working with a plane. I thought about was how much fun I was having with these planes on this material.

Nevertheless, you can form mouldings just as easily with a router as you can with moulding planes. That's the way I did it for many years.

Planning a Crown Moulding

I like to think of crown mouldings in three parts, each of which is formed from a separate piece of stock. The bottom element of the crown molding transitions down toward the cabinet. I used a Grecian ogee plane for this. Several ogee router bits could produce a similar effect. The next element, the one in the middle, I think of as the moulding's waist, and I frequently use a cove of some kind to create an appealing transition between the bottom and top elements of the moulding. For this particular crown molding, I used a No.7 round. For the top element in my moulding, I used a $^3/8$" (9mm) side bead. Here,

too, it's possible to create a similar effect using a bead-cutting router bit.

The secret, I think, to creating attractive crown moldings is experimentation. Run a few inches of mouldings using each of your router bits. Then assemble them in different configurations until you get one that looks right. Remember that you can get a very different effect by cutting the moulding on the side of your stock rather than on the edge. Here, too, experimentation is important.

If you choose to create the crown molding using hand planes as I did, read on for some suggestions.

The first thing you must do is create smooth edges perpendicular to the faces of the boards you're moulding. With conventional material, this can be done quite nicely on a jointer. However, when you're working with figured material, sometimes even a well-tuned jointer can produce tearout. This is work for which a good plane—like the infill panel plane in **Photo 1**—is well suited.

In **Photo 2**, you can see the three elements of my crown moulding, as well as the three tools that created those elements.

Most complex molders (planes that produce a shape with more than one

component) are sprung. That is, they are designed to work at an angle. The angle at which the plane is canted is indicated by a pair of crossed lines incised on the nose of the plane. One line representing vertical and the other representing horizontal **(Photo 3)**.

Rounds—like the one I used for my cove—don't have fences on their soles. They must be used against a batten (like the dado plane shown in step 4, page 29). In **photo 4**, I'm using a No. 7 round against a batten to create my cove.

The side bead is probably the easiest molding plane to master. It will quickly and efficiently cut a bead like the one you see in **Photo 5**. It needs no batten because its sole is equipped with a fence.

10 Use clamps to hold the large front section of the crown moulding in place while the glue dries. You can hand hold the two little ears of molding on either side for about 30 seconds until the glue sets.

11 Drill the shelf bracket holes.

13 On the back side of the door frame stock, cut a rabbet using a plane called a moving filletster. You can also make the rabbets using a dado cutter on the table saw or using a straight bit in a router.

12 Mill the door frames to the final thickness and width. Then, on the front of each piece, cut a bead with a ¼" (6mm) side-bead plane. This is a smaller version of the ⅜" (9mm) side bead I used on the top element of the cabinet's crown moulding. See "moulding-making options".

14 Cut the miters on the table saw and clean them up using a plane and a shooting board.

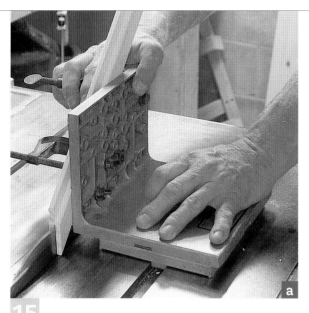 

15 Cut the notches for the feathers that hold the doors together. Then resaw the feather stock and plane it to nearly the exact thickness (it must be just a tad thinner in order to slide into the notches slathered with glue). Then mark and cut the feather stock to fit each of the notches.

16 The grain in the feather must run perpendicular to the miter joint it is crossing. If the grain runs parallel to the miter, the feather won't have any strength.

17 Make a clamping table to apply pressure to all four sides of the doors while the glued feathers cured. The table is a plywood surface with screwed blocks, each of which is a bit outside the limits of the door frame. Cut pairs of wedges to fit inside each of the blocks. By tapping the paired wedges together, pressure is applyed to all sides of the door while holding it squarely. (As an option, you can reinforce the joinery with flat brass corners screwed to the back side of the doors.)

18 Mark and cut each of the door hinge mortises.

19 Define the outline of the mortise and cut the sides to depth using a chisel.

20 Clean out the mortise using a chisel.

a b

21 Many years ago, I discovered the center punch and in an instant, my hinge installation improved dramatically. With this tool, you don't have to guess at the center of every screw hole on a hinge. The center punch finds the center, then punches a shallow depression that you can use to register the tip of your drill bit. In the photo at left, you can see the tapered tip of the center punch protruding through a screw hole in a hinge leaf. Because that tip is tapered, it automatically locates the center of the hole. In the photo at right, I'm using the punch to mark holes.

22 After you've installed the hinges on the doors, hold each door in place while you mark the location of the hinge mortises on the cabinet sides. Remove the hinges from the door. Holding each hinge in position on the cabinet side, mark around the hinge, then cut the mortises and install the hinges just as you did on the door frames.

23 Finally, add a little bead between the doors, recessing it just a bit. This detail, which I stole from many period originals, adds an appealing visual accent.

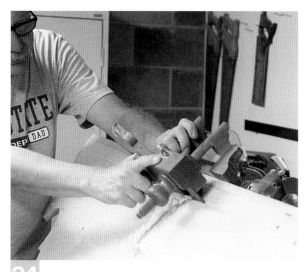

24 In order to hide the light cord, drill a hole in the cabinet top and another hole in the cabinet back. Then, on the back side of the cabinet back, plow a groove that intersects the drilled hole in the cabinet back. I cut this groove with a plow plane, but you might choose to cut it with a router and a straight bit.

After the cabinet is finished, mount the light, cut the plug from the light cord, feed the cord through the hole in the cabinet top, the hole in the cabinet back, and lay the cord in the plowed groove. The groove allows the cord to exit the cabinet at the very bottom. Then put a new plug on the cord.

25 Apply two coats of rub-on finish and fasten the glass door panels in place with a thin bead of clear silicone in the rabbets on the back of the door frame. Install the doors and the door hardware. Hang the cabinet from a pair of lag bolts that pass through holes in the tops of the two cabinet backs (these holes are hidden by the crown molding) and penetrate a pair of wall studs.

drop-leaf
kitchen table

4

This elegant little drop-leaf table is perfect for an eat-in kitchen or efficiency apartment. With its leaves raised, it's 48" (122cm) in diameter, but with both leaves dropped, it narrows to 24" (61cm) wide.

Installed in the base is a handy double-faced drawer that you can open from either side. Anything from silverware and placemats to hammers and pliers can be stored in the drawer.

The design of this table is simple but with enough style to fit almost anywhere. The base can be painted, as I have done, or it can be made of wood that matches the top and finished natural.

by Andy McCormick

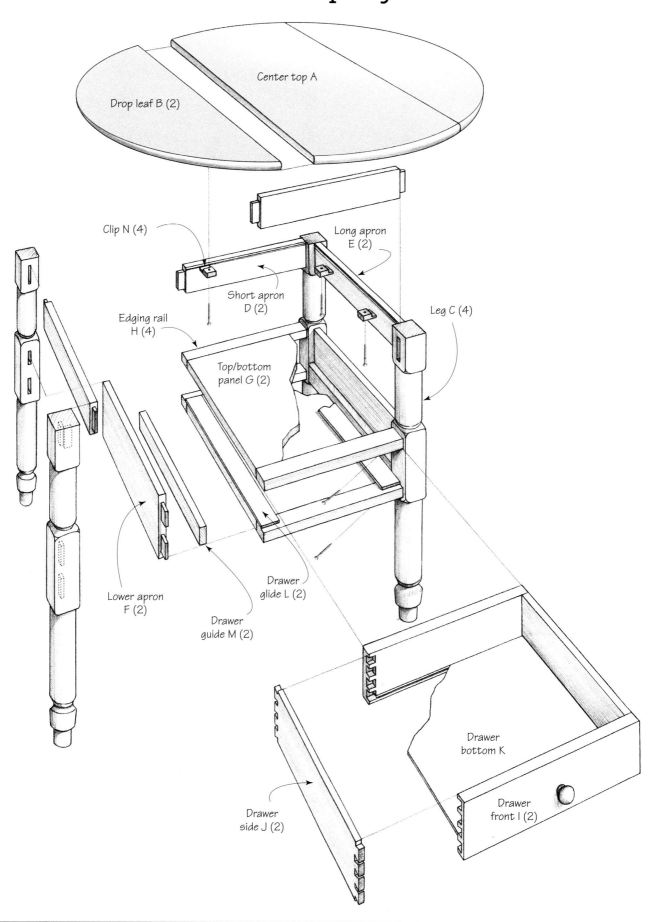

Center top A

Drop leaf B (2)

Clip N (4)

Long apron
E (2)

Short apron
D (2)

Edging rail
H (4)

Leg C (4)

Top/bottom
panel G (2)

Lower apron
F (2)

Drawer
guide M (2)

Drawer
glide L (2)

Drawer
bottom K

Drawer
side J (2)

Drawer
front I (2)

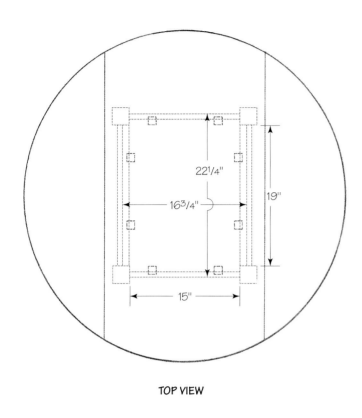

TOP VIEW

LEG DETAIL

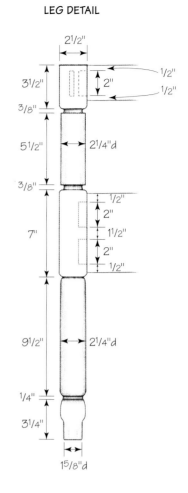

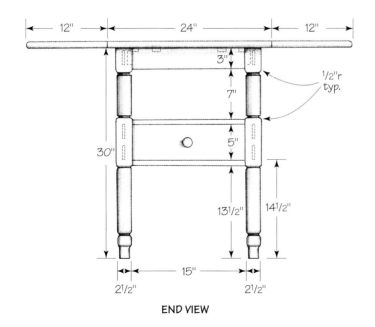

END VIEW

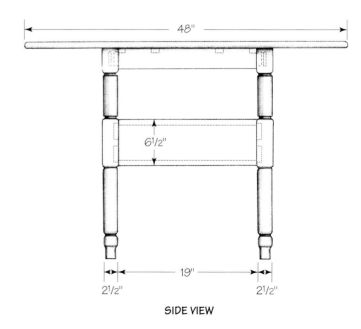

SIDE VIEW

CUTTING LIST ■ *dropleaf kitchen table* inches (millimeters)

REFERENCE	QUANTITY	PART	STOCK	THICKNESS		WIDTH		LENGTH		COMMENTS
A	1	center top	cherry	³/₄-⁷/₈	(19-22)	24	(610)	48	(1219)	
B	2	drop leaves	cherry	³/₄-⁷/₈	(19-22)	12	(305)	48	(1219)	
C	4	legs	poplar	2¹/₂	(64)	2¹/₂	(64)	30	(762)	
D	2	short aprons	poplar	³/₄	(19)	3	(76)	16¹/₂	(419)	length includes ³/₄" (19mm)-lo tenons on both ends
E	2	long aprons	poplar	³/₄	(19)	3	(76)	20¹/₂	(521)	length includes ³/₄" (19mm)-lo tenons on both ends
F	2	lower aprons	poplar	³/₄	(19)	6¹/₂	(165)	20¹/₂	(521)	length includes ³/₄" (19mm)-lo double tenons on both ends
G	2	top and bottom panels	birch plywood	³/₄	(19)	16³/₄	(425)	19	(483)	
H	4	edging rails	poplar	³/₄	(19)	2	(51)	15	(381)	
I	2	drawer fronts	poplar	³/₄	(19)	4³/₄	(121)	14³/₄	(375)	
J	2	drawer sides	poplar	¹/₂	(13)	4³/₄	(121)	21⁷/₈	(556)	
K	1	drawer bottom	birch plywood	¹/₄	(6)	14¹/₄	(362)	22	(559)	
L	2	drawer glides	poplar	¹/₈	(3)	2	(51)	19	(483)	
M	2	drawer guides	poplar	1	(25)	2	(51)	19	(483)	
N	4	clips	poplar	³/₄	(19)	1	(25)	2	(51)	

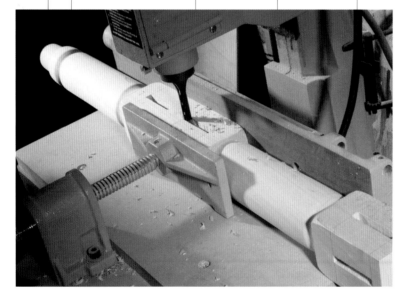

hardware & supplies
- 1 pair—metal drop-leaf supports
- 2 pair—drop-leaf hinges
- No. 20 biscuits
- 4—No. 8 × 1" (25mm) wood screws
- paint for base
- stain
- clear finish

1 After turning the legs to shape, cut the mortise slots. This can also be done with a router and a jig, a router mounted under a router table or a drill press with a Forstner bit followed by cleanup with a chisel.

a b

2 Cut the cheeks for the tenons first.

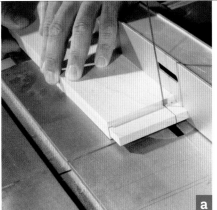

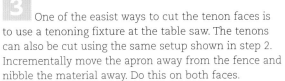

3 One of the easist ways to cut the tenon faces is to use a tenoning fixture at the table saw. The tenons can also be cut using the same setup shown in step 2. Incrementally move the apron away from the fence and nibble the material away. Do this on both faces.

4 The band saw is great for cutting the tenon offset. Complete the offset by cutting the scrap away with a hand saw.

6 Make sure you do the leg assembly glue-ups on a flat surface so everything stays flat. Also, check for squareness. (If everything has been cut properly, the sides should go together perfectly.)

7 Using the short aprons, attach the two base side assemblies to-gether.

5 When the mortises and tenons have been cut and dry fitted, assemble the two sides of the base.

8 Using glue, pocket holes and screws, attach the top of the drawer box.

9 Using glue and pockets screws, attach two edging rails to each end of the top of the drawer box.

10 Attach the bottom of the drawer box and two edging rails to the table base using the same method shown in steps 8 and 9.

11 Attach the drawer guides using glue and nails. Note that the guide is about 1/16" (2mm) proud of the inside faces of the legs. This will keep the drawer fronts from hitting the legs.

12 Install the drawer glides with glue. The glides automatically create the proper gap between the bottom of the drawer front and the bottom of the drawer box. These glides also help the drawer glide smoothly.

13 The drawer sides (left) are dovetailed into the drawer fronts (right). I cut these dovetails using a router jig and a router setup with a dovetail bit. They're not fancy but they are strong and look good when the drawers are assembled.

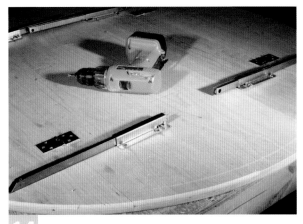

14 Glue up enough hardwood boards to create the proper widths needed for the center top and the two drop-leaves. Then attach the parts to each other using drop-leaf hinges. Install the drop-leaf supports.

15 Using a router setup with a roundover bit, cut a roundover on the bottom and top edges of the tabletop. A chamfer instead of a roundover also looks good.

16 The top is attached to the base using wooden clips that you can make on the table saw. After making sure that all is working properly, remove the top from the base. Now you can paint or stain the base and finish the top. Reattach the top and you're ready to sit down to a well deserved meal.

43

Though it has no specific antecedent, this round occasional table displays common country motifs: simple tapered legs, scroll-cut aprons and a painted finish. Its size and height makes it adaptable for a variety of uses.

The tapered legs are slightly splayed to increase the table's stability, but their feet don't reach beyond the perimeter of the tabletop. The aprons, whose ends are cut at a slight angle, produce the splay. The shelf is captured in notches sawed into the legs.

The router figures prominently in the table's construction. The mortises are cut with a plunge router, and both the tabletop and shelf are cut with a router and trammel. The aprons' scrollwork is refined with a router and template.

5

lamp table

Built a couple of centuries ago, this country table would have been painted from bottom to top. In the ensuing decades, daily use would have worn the paint off the top's surface and the edges of the shelf. Rather than mimic the wear of time, the stand is painted and the white oak top has a durable varnish finish.

The tabletop is made of white oak, a widely available domestic hardwood. It's attractive and durable and, because the stock is quarter-sawn rather than flat-sawn, it moves less in width and is likely to hold its roundness through the seasons. The stand is built of poplar, a low-cost, widely available hardwood that works easily and takes paint well.

by Bill Hylton

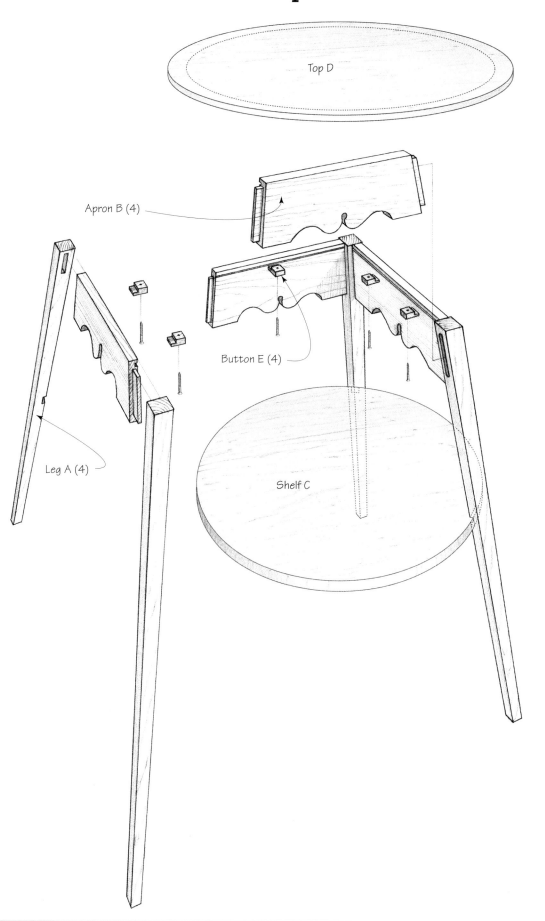

Top D

Apron B (4)

Button E (4)

Leg A (4)

Shelf C

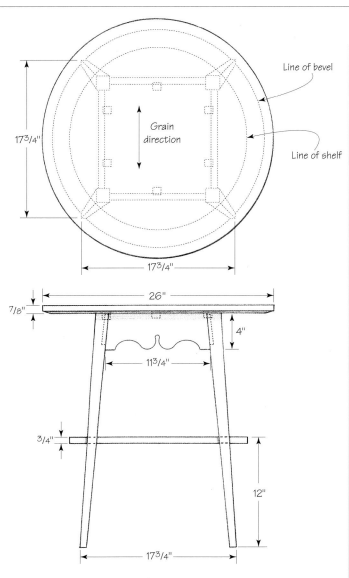

Line of bevel

Line of shelf

Grain direction

17³/4"

17³/4"

26"

7/8"

4"

11³/4"

3/4"

12"

17³/4"

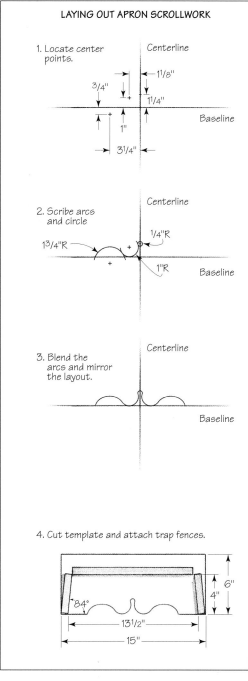

LAYING OUT APRON SCROLLWORK

1. Locate center points.

Centerline

3/4"

1¹/8"

1¹/4"

Baseline

1"

3¹/4"

2. Scribe arcs and circle

Centerline

1³/4"R

1/4"R

1"R

Baseline

3. Blend the arcs and mirror the layout.

Centerline

Baseline

4. Cut template and attach trap fences.

6"

4"

84°

13¹/2"

15"

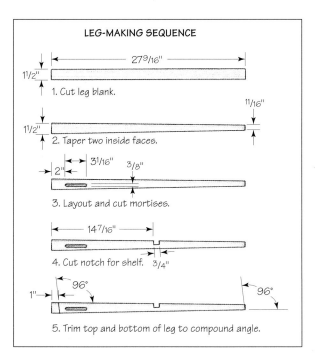

LEG-MAKING SEQUENCE

27⁹/16"

1¹/2"

1. Cut leg blank.

1¹/16"

1¹/2"

2. Taper two inside faces.

2"

3¹/16"

3/8"

3. Layout and cut mortises.

14⁷/16"

4. Cut notch for shelf.   3/4"

1"

96°

96°

5. Trim top and bottom of leg to compound angle.

CUTTING LIST ■ *lamp table* inches (millimeters)

REFERENCE	QUANTITY	PART	STOCK	THICKNESS		WIDTH		LENGTH		COMMENTS
A	4	legs	poplar	1½	(38)	1½	(38)	27½	(699)	will be cut to 26½" (673mm) during construction
B	4	aprons	poplar	⅞	(22)	4¼	(108)	13½	(343)	width be cut to 3⅞" (98mm) during construction
C	1	shelf	poplar	¾	(19)	24	(610)	24	(610)	final diameter of shelf determined during construction
D	1	top	white oak	13/16	(21)	28	(711)	28	(711)	cut 26" (660mm) diameter top from glued-up panel
E	6	buttons	poplar	¾	(19)	⅞	(22)	1¼	(32)	

hardware & supplies

- 6—No. 6 × 1¼" (30mm) wood screws
- paint for table base
- clear finish for tabletop

1 Crosscut 12/4 stock to about 2" (51mm) longer than the leg length specified on the cutting list. Face joint and plane the stock the minimum needed to create flat parallel faces. Joint an edge and rip the stock into four oversize blanks. Cut a 1⅝" (41mm) square window in a piece of cardboard and use this template to lay out a leg on the end grain of each oversize blank. Orient the layout so the annular rings (marked by the red line in the photo) run diagonally.

2 Rip the individual legs from the oversize blanks with the blade tilted to match the angle of the layout. Since the layout orientation on each blank is likely to be different, you'll have to adjust the tilt (and the fence position) for each blank. Place the blank behind the blade and tilt the blade until it aligns with the layout. Then set the fence so the cut will align with the layout.

3 Make the bevel cut, creating a base surface so the three remaining rips can all be made with the blade square to the saw's table. Since the degree of blade-tilt needed for this cut will likely vary from blank to blank, you'll need to set up for each cut individually. Make this cut on each blank before making the squaring cuts.

4 Reset the blade square to the table and make a second cut on each blank. You'll have to reposition the rip fence to align this cut against the individual lay-outs. After making a second cut on each blank, set the fence at 1⅝" (41mm) and make all the remaining cuts.

5 Taper the legs. There are several ways to do this. I suggest doing it with a simple fixture (shown at left) on the table saw. Once you've made the jig, sawing the tapers is a matter of two rip cuts per leg. Set the first leg in the jig and secure it with the clamp. Set the rip fence to accommodate the narrow end of the jig with the leg. Feed the jig and leg along the fence. Because the jig holds the leg at an angle to the blade, you'll rip a taper. Loosen the clamp and rotate the leg 90° to the right (so the just cut face is up). Repeat the cut, tapering the adjacent face. In the same way, make two cuts on each of the remaining three legs. As you taper the legs, save the wedges of waste; you'll use them when you glue up the stand.

6 Cut the mortises. You can do this job with a hollow-chisel mortiser, but I used a plunge router, edge guide and a shopmade jig. The fixture holds the leg and supports the router. The router's plunge controls the final depth and the edge guide positions the cut. Stops on the fixture limit the length of the cut. Because of the leg's taper, the mortises are slighter deeper at the upper end than the lower one, and that's OK.

7 Lay out a mortise on one leg, as shown in the photo; use this sample to set up the fixture and router. Mark the other mortise locations only with the registration line, which corresponds to the middle of the cut. Once the equipment is set up, all mortises will be identical as long as you clamp the leg in the fixture with the untapered faces against the workrest and the fixture back, with the line on the leg aligned with the fixture's registration line. The leg extends left for some mortises and right for others.

8 Notch each leg for the round shelf using dado cutter. Set it up to perfectly match the thickness of the shelf stock and tilt to 6°. Cradle the leg in a V-block so the cut is in the arris of the leg and guide the leg across the cutter with the miter gauge. When you set up, position the V-block so it grazes the cutter. Clamp it to the miter gauge.

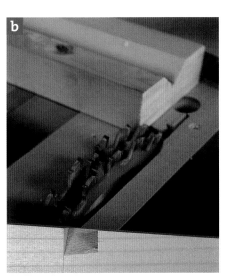

9 Set the mark you made on the leg during your original layout at the end of the block. Make the first cut in the first leg with the cutter deliberately set low. Measure the result and raise the cutter so the resulting cut is ³⁄₈" (10mm)-deep. Cut each leg.

10 Trim leg tops to the layout marks. The cut is a compound angle with a 6° bevel and a 6° miter.

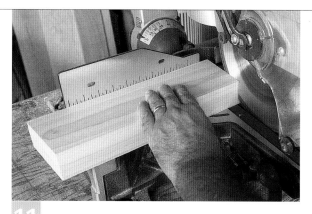

11 Prepare the stock for the aprons. Joint and plane it to the specified thickness, rip it to width and crosscut four pieces slightly longer than the finished size. Reduce them to the desired length as you miter the ends. Here, a pair of aprons are being mitered at one time.

12 Lay out the apron contour on a piece of hardboard, following the drawing "Laying Out Apron Scrollwork" on page 47. Begin with a piece that's 8" (203mm) × 15" (381mm). Lay out the full contour, then cut it out. Drill the center hole first with a $1/2$" (13mm) Forstner bit. With a jigsaw, saw as close to the line as possible. Smooth the contour with coarse sandpaper or a half-round file.

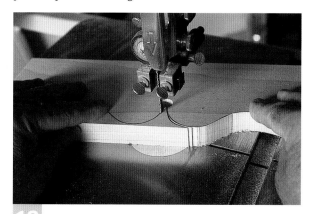

13 Use the template as a pattern to mark the contour on each apron (trace along the template edge with a pencil). Take the four aprons to the drill press and bore the center hole in each one with the $1/2$" (13mm) Forstner bit. Take them to the band saw next and saw just outside the traced line on each, roughing out the contour.

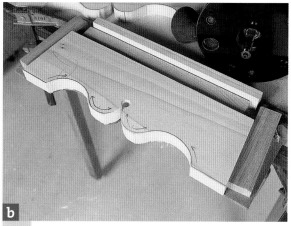

a

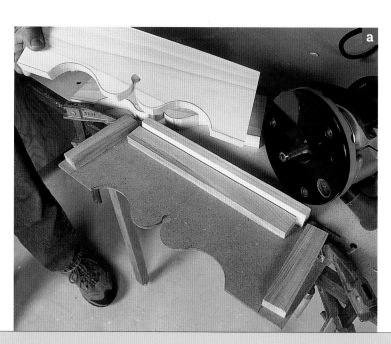

b

14 Set up the template by clamping it so the guiding edge overhangs the workbench. Install a flush-trimming bit in your router and adjust the bit extension so the pilot bearing on the tip rides along the template when the router is resting on top of the workpiece. Before you rout any of the aprons, look at the arrows penciled on the apron in the photo. Given the rotation of the bit, you risk splitting a chunk off the convex shape if you move the router "uphill" across the grain. To prevent this, always move the router so the bit is cutting "downhill" across the grain. Follow the arrows, in other words. Yes, you'll be climb cutting portions of the contour, but you shouldn't have any trouble controlling the router.

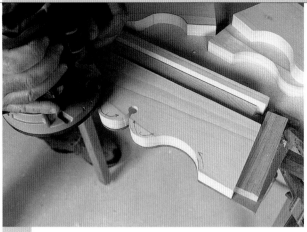

15 Set an apron on the template. The fences force the workpiece into the right position and prevent it from moving. The router holds it down as you cut. Rest the tool on the work with the bit clear of the edge. Switch it on and trim the work's edge flush with the template edge. Be mindful of the appropriate direction to move the router. Because of the narrow passage at the center of the control, you won't be able to address the entire contour. Use a file to smooth the edges you can't get to with the router bit.

16 Form the cheeks of the tenons on the router table. The best bit to use is a large-diameter mortising bit (intended for routing recesses for hinge leaves) or a bottom-cleaning bit. A large-diameter straight bit will work too. As you creep up on the optimum depth of cut, make test-cuts on scraps of the apron stock and fit the resulting tenons to a mortise in one of the legs. Set the fence of the router-table produce the correct tenon length. To cut a tenon cheek, butt the apron end against the fence and slide it along the fence and across the bit. You can cut the full depth in a single pass.

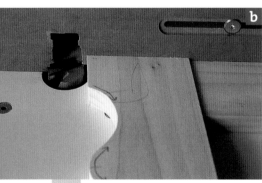

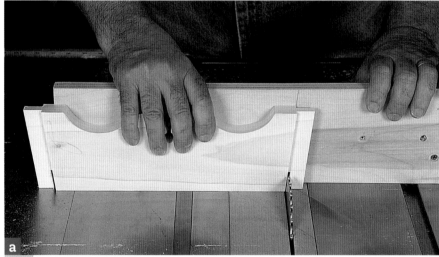

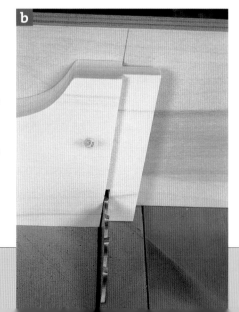

17 Use a scrap as a pusher to back up the stock edge and prevent tear-out. Because the aprons are mitered at a 6° angle, you must miter the end of the pusher as well. Orient the pusher so its end is in full contact with the edge of the workpiece. When you turn the apron over, you also must turn over the pusher.

18 The mortise-and-tenon joint has a deep shoulder at the top. The cleanest way to cut this shoulder is on the table saw. Elevate the blade 1" (25mm) and tilt it 6°. Attach a facing to the miter gauge that's taller than the apron width. Kerf the facing and extend a line from the kerf to the top of the facing. Stand the apron on its top edge and align the tenon shoulder at the line (inset). Kerf the tenon. Turn the apron around, align the shoulder with the line and kerf the second tenon. Cut these shoulders on all four aprons.

19 With a square, lay out the edge cuts—one at the top and one at the bottom. The cuts should be perpendicular to the tenon shoulder. Make the cuts on the band saw.

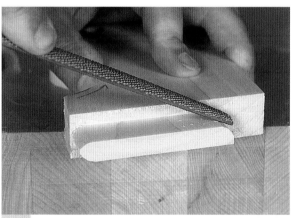

20 The ends of the mortises are rounded, so round off the tenon corners with a pattern-maker's rasp. Be careful not to nick the tenon shoulders with the rasp.

21 The final step is to chamfer the inside corner of each tenon. The mortises in each leg intersect. To allow the tenons to penetrate the mortises fully, you have to trim them slightly. The task can be done with a chisel or block plane. I chucked a chamfer bit in the router table to do the job uniformly.

22 Glue up two legs and one apron. Use the wedges you made when you tapered the legs as clamping cauls. Apply a pipe clamp across the outside of the assembly, along the top edge of the apron. Turn the assembly over and apply a second clamp along the bottom edge of the apron. Assemble the other two legs to an apron in the same way.

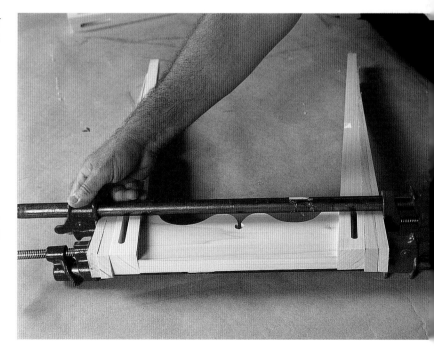

23 After the glue sets, dry assemble the two subassemblies with the remaining two aprons. (Use masking tape to attach the cauls to the legs, so you don't need an extra pair of hands to apply the clamps.) With a yardstick or folding rule, measure diagonally from shelf-notch to shelf-notch. The distance is the diameter of shelf you need.

24 With a router and trammel, cut the shelf to the desired diameter. Set the shelf blank, bottom-side up, on an expendable piece of plywood or hardboard and clamp it at two corners to the workbench. Locate the pivot and drill a shallow hole for the pivot screw. Set the router's plunge depth to no more than $1/16$" (2mm) more than the shelf thickness. Adjust the trammel for the radius of the cut (the bit should be outside the radius). Attach the trammel at the pivot point and cut the shelf. You'll need four to six passes to cut through the stock without overtaxing your router and bit.

25 After the shelf is sanded and ready for final assembly, make a practice run. Don't open the glue until you have the cauls taped to the legs, the clamp jaws set and you know—because you've tried it—that everything fits together.

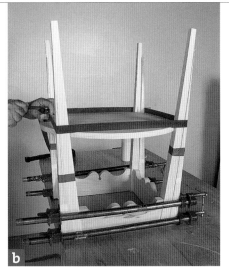

26 Lay a leg-and-apron subassembly on the bench. Apply glue to the mortises and tenons and fit the two remaining aprons to the subassembly. Apply glue to the shelf notches. Set the shelf into the notches. Apply glue to the mortises in the second leg-and-apron subassembly, to its shelf notches and to the exposed tenons of the aprons. Set the second subassembly in place using a dead-blow mallet to seat it. Tip the assembly upside down and apply pipe clamps. Then drop a band clamp over the legs and tighten it to pull the legs tight against the shelf.

27 Cut the table with the router and trammel, the same way you did the shelf. The only differences are the size and the stock.

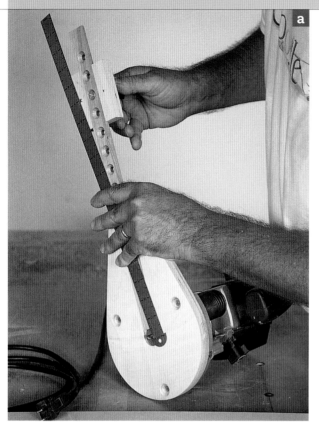

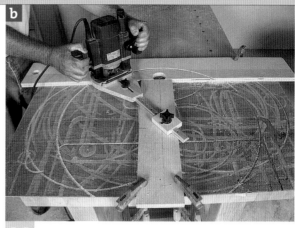

28 Make a curved fence to use for beveling the underside of the tabletop. Cut the bevel with a horizontal panel-raising bit, which should be used only in a router table. Because you want only the bevel and not the tongue, you can't guide the cut with the bit's pilot bearing, hence the fence. Though the radius of the fence's curve is the same as the tabletop's, the bit must be inside the radius, so the trammel's pivot must be readjusted. Clamp the fence across the bench on top of the sacrificial plywood. Locate the pivot for the arc you need to cut, clamp a scrap there and attach the trammel pivot to it. Rout the arc.

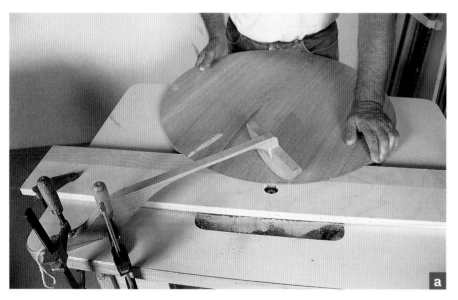

29 Bevel the underside of the tabletop. Install a straight-bevel panel raiser in your router table. Clamp the fence to the table. (You'll need to bore a clearance hole in the fence for the pilot bearing.) Make sure the fence is positioned to eliminate the tongue-forming portion of the bit; you want only the bevel. A hold-down to help you keep the work tight to the table is useful, but the setup doesn't accommodate the featherboards. The hold-down I used looks odd but works great. To cut, turn on the router with the work clear of the bit. When the bit is up to speed, push the tabletop against the work and move it counterclockwise. A chalk mark can serve as a benchmark, so you know when you've turned the work a full 360°. It's a good idea to stage the cut, starting with a shallow cut and achieving the full depth on the third pass.

30 Cut grooves in the aprons for the mounting buttons. You do this now because the aprons are canted, and it is simply easier to groove them after the stand is already assembled. Attach your router to a long plywood strip that will span the stand. (You can mount it temporarily with carpet tape.) Use a $^1/_4$" (6mm) slot cutter. Adjust the cutter so the top edge of the groove is $^5/_8$" (16mm) from the top edge of the stand. Cut a single slot into two aprons and two slots into each of the others.

31 Make the buttons. Select a wide piece of $^3/_4$" (19mm) thick stock and cut a $^1/_2$" wide (13mm) by $^9/_{16}$" deep (14mm) rabbet across each end. Cut a strip $1^1/_4$" (32mm) long from each end of the board, then cut the strip into $^7/_8$" (22mm)-wide buttons. Drill a pilot hole through the center of each.

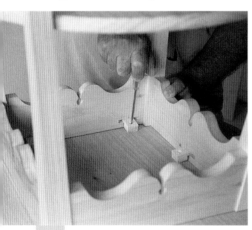

32 Mount the tabletop before applying a finish. Set the tabletop, top surface down, on the bench top. Upend the stand and line it up on the tabletop. Fit a button into each slot you cut. Use an awl to locate pilot holes for buttons. Remove the stand, and drill the pilot holes.

33 I finished the top and the stand separately. The tabletop received several coats of rub-on finish. Between coats, I buffed with No.0000 steel wool. I rubbed out the final coat with paste wax and steel wool. I primed the stand with dewaxed shellac, then applied two coats of oil-base paint.

dining table

6

The focus of a well-designed dining room is most often the dining room table. It should be stout and pleasurable to the eye —an invitation to enjoy a family event. The Pilgrim-style table is just that piece. I enjoy the way the stained top bounces off the black painted base, which is plenty strong and solid to support such frivolity.

The hefty turned legs, with the H-stretcher base support, will withstand centuries of use and the beaded apron adds a bit of charm to the design. As for the top, this is the area to use your selection of hardwoods to raise the table to superb status.

I originally built this table for a customer who, while searching through a copy of Wallace Nutting's *Furniture Treasury*, froze because he knew he had found the perfect focus for his setting. You should experience that feeling in your dining room.

by Glen Huey

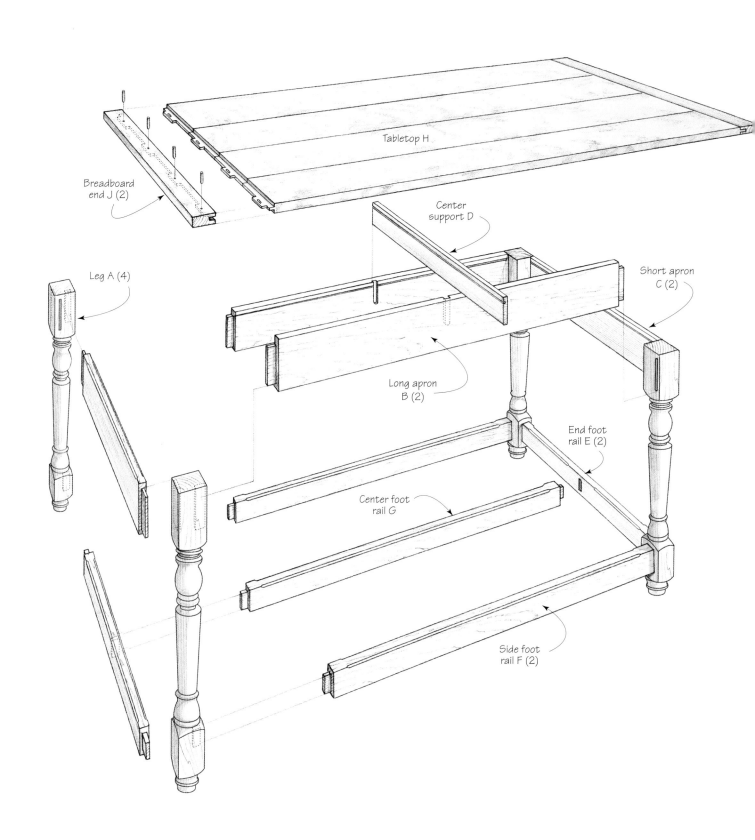

Breadboard
end J (2)

Tabletop H

Center
support D

Leg A (4)

Short apron
C (2)

Long apron
B (2)

End foot
rail E (2)

Center foot
rail G

Side foot
rail F (2)

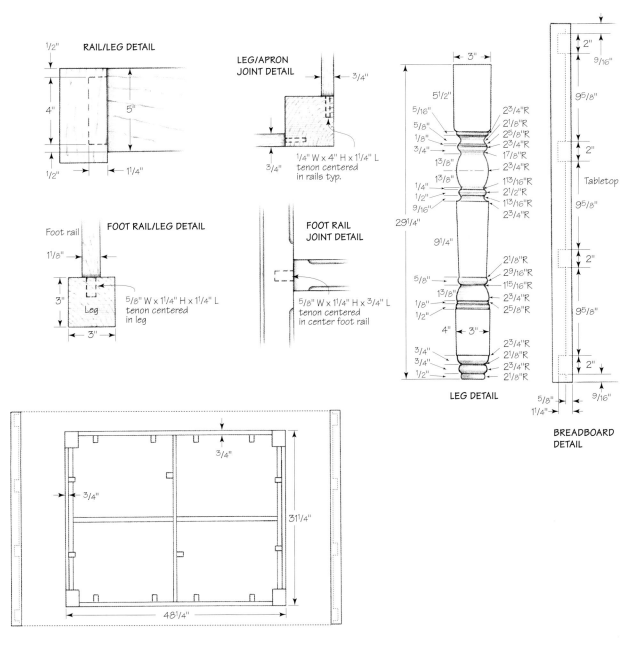

RAIL/LEG DETAIL

1/2"
4"
5"
1/2"
1 1/4"

LEG/APRON
JOINT DETAIL

3/4"
3/4"

1/4" W x 4" H x 1 1/4" L
tenon centered
in rails typ.

FOOT RAIL/LEG DETAIL

Foot rail
1 1/8"
3"
Leg
3"

5/8" W x 1 1/4" H x 1 1/4" L
tenon centered
in leg

FOOT RAIL
JOINT DETAIL

5/8" W x 1 1/4" H x 3/4" L
tenon centered
in center foot rail

LEG DETAIL

3"
5 1/2"
5/16"
5/8"
1/8"
3/4"
1 3/8"
1 3/8"
1/4"
1/2"
9/16"
29 1/4"
9 1/4"
5/8"
1 3/8"
1/8"
1/2"
4"   3"
3/4"
3/4"
1/2"

2 3/4"R
2 1/8"R
2 5/8"R
2 3/4"R
1 7/8"R
2 3/4"R
1 13/16"R
2 1/2"R
1 13/16"R
2 3/4"R
2 1/8"R
2 9/16"R
1 15/16"R
2 3/4"R
2 5/8"R
2 3/4"R
2 1/8"R
2 3/4"R
2 1/8"R

BREADBOARD
DETAIL

2"
9/16"
9 5/8"
2"
Tabletop
9 5/8"
2"
9 5/8"
2"
5/8"
1 1/4"
9/16"

3/4"
3/4"
31 1/4"
48 1/4"

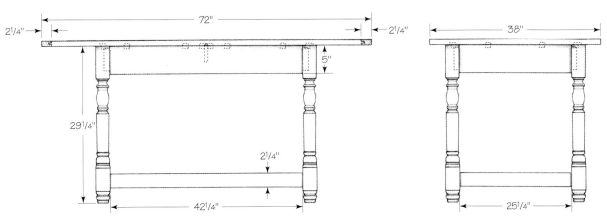

2 1/4"   72"   2 1/4"
5"
29 1/4"
2 1/4"
42 1/4"

38"
25 1/4"

CUTTING LIST ■ *dining table* inches (millimeters)

REFERENCE	QUANTITY	PART	STOCK	THICKNESS		WIDTH		LENGTH		COMMENTS
A	4	legs	poplar	3	(76)	3	(76)	29¼	(743)	
B	2	long aprons	poplar	¾	(19)	5	(127)	44¾	(1137)	1¼" (32mm) tenon both ends
C	2	short aprons	poplar	¾	(19)	5	(127)	27¾	(705)	1¼" (32mm) tenon both ends
D	1	center support	poplar	¾	(19)	5	(127)	30½	(775)	ends set into mortises in long aprons
E	2	end foot rails	poplar	1⅛	(286)	2¼	(57)	27¾	(705)	1¼" (32mm) tenon both ends, mortise in middl
F	2	side foot rails	poplar	1⅛	(286)	2¼	(57)	44¾	(1137)	1¼" (32mm) tenon both ends, mortise in middl
G	1	center foot rail	poplar	1⅛	(286)	2¼	(57)	47½	(1207)	⅜" (19mm) tenon both ends
H	1	tabletop	birch	¾	(19)	38	(965)	70	(1778)	1¼" (32mm) tenon both ends
J	2	breadboard ends	birch	¾	(19)	2¼	(57)	38	(965)	
K	14	wooden clips	poplar	¾	(19)	⅞	(22)	2¼	(57)	

hardware & supplies

- 8 ¼" (6mm) square × 1½" (38mm) red oak pegs
- 14 No. 8 × 1¼" (30mm) flathead wood screws
- paint for base
- stain
- clear finish for top

1 The legs are each two pieces of 8/4 material that are milled to 1½" (38mm) × 3" (76mm), then glued together to a finished size of 3" (76mm) square. They are then turned to the profile provided in the plans. Once turned, you can layout the mortises: two in each leg on adjacent face sides of the upper blocks. The mortises are ¼" (6mm) wide by 4" (102mm) long by 1¼" (32mm) deep and located ⅝" (16mm) on center from the outer faces of the legs. Use the step method to cut the mortises: cut ¼" (6mm) square holes about ³⁄₁₆" (5mm) apart. Then, go back and remove the bridged sections to complete the mortises. Cut one mortise, flip the leg end for end, rotate it 90° and cut the other mortise.

2 Layout the mortises for the foot rail ends. These will be centered in the lower leg block and are ⅝" (16mm) wide × 1¾" (44mm) long × 1¼" (32mm) deep. There is only one per leg. I changed the mortise set to a ½" (13mm) chisel and bit to make the job quicker. In the center of the foot rail ends, cut a ⅝"-wide × 1¾"-long × ¾"-deep (16mm × 44mm × 19mm) mortise to accept the center foot rail.

cutting the tenon

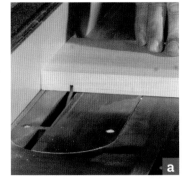
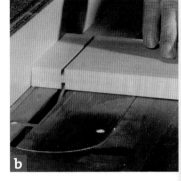
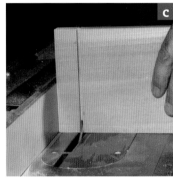
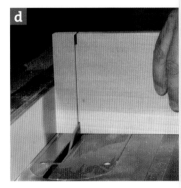

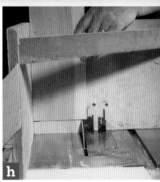

finished tenon

■ defining the shoulder (a-d)

Once the legs are complete, you will need to begin the work on the aprons and foot rails. Mill the material to size according to the cutting list, set the table saw so the blade is $\frac{1}{4}$" (6mm) high and the fence is $1\frac{1}{8}$" (29mm) from the blade. Make a pass over the blade, cutting each face of the apron and foot rail end (photos a and b). Without changing the fence position, raise the blade to $\frac{1}{2}$" (13mm) and make the cut on the edges of the apron pieces (photos c and d)

■ shaping the cheeks (e-g)

Turn of the saw and raise the blade to the top edge of the shoulder cuts (photo e). If you make the cut too low you will have to remove some material by hand. If the cut is set too high, gaps will show after the pieces are in place on the table base. Use a tenoning fixture (mine is homemade, shown in photo f) to make the cheek cuts on the aprons and foot rails. The aprons have $1\frac{1}{4}$"-long (32mm) tenons and the long foot rail has $\frac{3}{4}$"-long (19mm) tenons. Also, the aprons have $\frac{1}{4}$"-thick (6mm) tenons and the end and long foot rails have $\frac{5}{8}$"-thick (16mm) tenons. Make one pass, allowing the waste to drop from the outer edge of the cut, then reverse the piece and make the second cut, again allowing the waste to fall from the outer face of the tenon. Fit the tenons snugly into the mortises. They must be snug because this creates the holding power of the joint.

■ cutting tenon to width (h-i)

Cut the tenons to width using the fixture. Don't worry about getting a tight fit for the width of the tenons. I like to be able to slide the tenon up or down when aligning it in the final position.

4 Use a handheld router or a table-mounted router to cut the 1/4" (6mm) beading on the edges of the aprons.

5 I used a 3/16" (5mm) roundover bit to ease the top edges of the foot rails, stopping 1" (25mm) from the rail-to-leg, rail-to-post or center-rail-to-end joints.

6 Apply glue into the mortises and onto the tenons of the short aprons and foot rail ends. Slide the joints together, clamp and allow to dry. Assemble both end units.

7 Join the end assemblies together by attaching the long aprons and long foot rail to each end assembly.

9 Use a marking gauge set to 1¼" (32mm) to mark the four edges of the top.

8 The two base ends are connected using the aprons and foot rail. This table base will last for generations.

10

Clamp a straightedge in position to guide the router bit. Leave the scribe line exposed on the underside and just cover the line on the top side. This will result in a breadboard that is tight on the face side of the tabletop. Use a router with a $3/4$" (19mm) pattern bit set to leave a $1/4$" (6mm) tongue on the end of the tabletop [depth of cut will be $1/4$" (6mm) on a $3/4$"-thick (19mm) top]. Begin by climb-cutting (moving the router backwards) the end of each tongue. This will prevent the wood from tearing out. Finish the cut by moving the router from left to right. Flip the top and make the second cut.

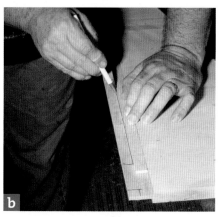

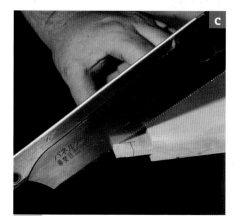

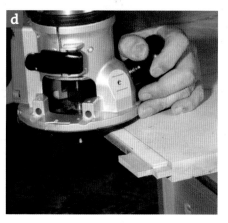

11

Layout and cut the multiple tenons. Locate the wide tenon areas using the layout guide in the plans (Photo a). Connect the tenons with a line that represents the tongue (Photo b). I used a hand saw to make the outside corner notch cuts. The crosscuts for the notch should line up with the bottom of the mortise in the breadboard end (Photo c). Use a jigsaw to remove most of the waste between the tenons. Remove the rest of the waste using a router with a straight-cutting bit that has a flush-cut bearing. Use a strip of wood that is the same width as the length of the tongue as a guide for the router bit (Photo d).

12

Set the table saw blade to the height of the length of the tabletop tongue, and cut a groove slightly off-center in the breadboard ends. Reverse the piece and make a second pass. This will ensure that the groove is located in the exact center of the piece. Test the fit of the mortise and adjust the cut as necessary. The mortise should fit snugly over the tenon ends.

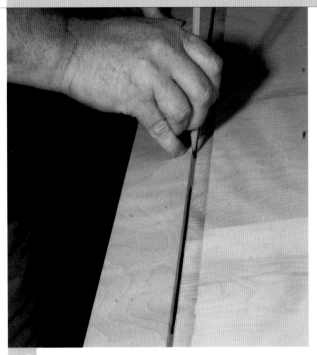

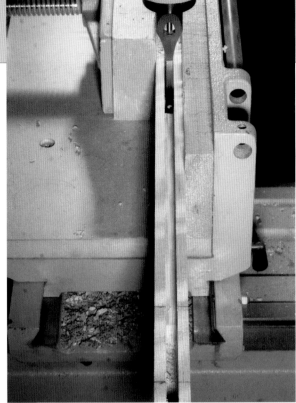

6

13 Position the breadboard onto the tenons and transfer the locations of the tenons onto the breadboard. I make a mark about ⅛" (3mm) wide of the tenon on each side. This slightly larger mortise will allow for expansion and contraction of the top within the confines of the breadboard ends.

14 Cut the mortises for the tabletop tenons using the mortiser.

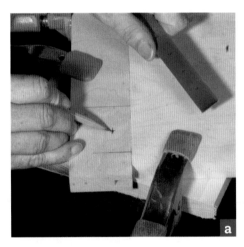

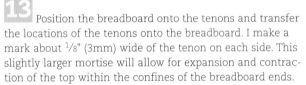

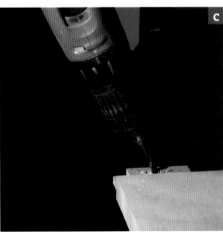

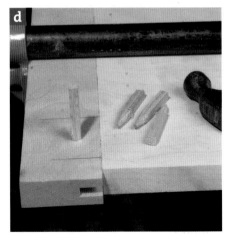

15 Install the wooden pegs. Slide the breadboard ends into the ends of the top and add clamps. Make sure the joint is tight. Use spring clamps to hold a scrap of wood (this will keep the hole clean on the bottom as the drill plunges through) on the underside of the tenon area. Mark and drill holes centered on the tenons (Photos a and b). Remove the breadboard ends and "rock" the drill to elongate each of the holes in the tenons (Photo c). Attach the breadboard to the tabletop by applying glue to the center 5" (127mm) of the breadboard's mortise. Then drive square pegs into the holes (Photo d). Use a denser hardwood for the pegs than you used on the tabletop. This will allow the hole to form to the squared pegs instead of vice versa.

16 Apply a water-based aniline dye to the tabletop. The color on this top is a mixture of 50 percent Golden Amber Maple and 50 percent Brown Walnut (mix the colors after they are in liquid form). After the stain is dry, sand the top with 400-grit wet/dry sandpaper to smooth the grain. Then, if using figured hardwood, apply a coat of boiled linseed oil. The oil will penetrate into the figured grain and highlight characteristics. After the oil has dried completely, apply a coat of shellac to seal the top. Sand the shellac with 400-grit sandpaper and apply two coats of precatalyzed lacquer using a high-volume-low-pressure (HVLP) spray gun.

17 The painting process for the table base is the same for the entertainment center project. After the paint is dry, appy a coat of a linseed oil and wax mixture to add durability and sheen.

18 The tabletop is attached to the base with 14 wooden clips. The clips have a ¼" (6mm) tongue that extends into a matching groove cut into the base aprons using a biscuit joiner. A single No. 8 × 1¼" (30mm) wood screw in each clip holds the top tightly in place.

Bedrooms in 18th-and 19th-century homes were often quite large with 9' (2.75m) or 10' (3m) ceilings. They were, therefore, appropriate settings for the also quite large four-post beds of the period. By contrast, contemporary bedrooms are smaller with typical ceiling heights of less than 8' (2.4m). Contemporary homes are, therefore, less comfortable settings for grand period or country four-post beds.

The master bedroom at my house is even smaller than those in most contemporary homes. It measures 11' (3.4m) × 12' (3.65m) with 7' 3" (2.2m) ceilings, so when my wife asked for a four-post bed, I realized I would have to design one with modest dimensions.

My wife and I began the project by looking through some furniture books. I did a little sketching, and we settled on a fully turned post with

7 pencil-post bed

a country rather than a period flavor, one embellished by a simple arrangement of beads, coves and vases.

If you're interested in building this four-post bed—or anything else that requires a distance between lathe centers of more than 36" (91cm)—put some thought into how you might lengthen the bed on your lathe. Even if it isn't a tubular bed lathe like mine, it's likely that there are techniques you can employ.

The posts on this particular piece of furniture are designed so that turners with access to only short-bed lathes can still produce them by turning each one in two segments. The two segments are later joined with a ¾" (19mm) turned tenon in the top of one segment which fits into a ¾" (19mm) mortise drilled into the bottom of the other segment. (See the construction notes for details.) This two-part construction works well because all the joinery is cut into the bottom portion of the post, below the location of the mortise-and-tenon joint. As a result, the mortise-and-tenon joint isn't load bearing.

by Kerry Pierce

CONSTRUCTION NOTES ▪ *pencil-post bed*

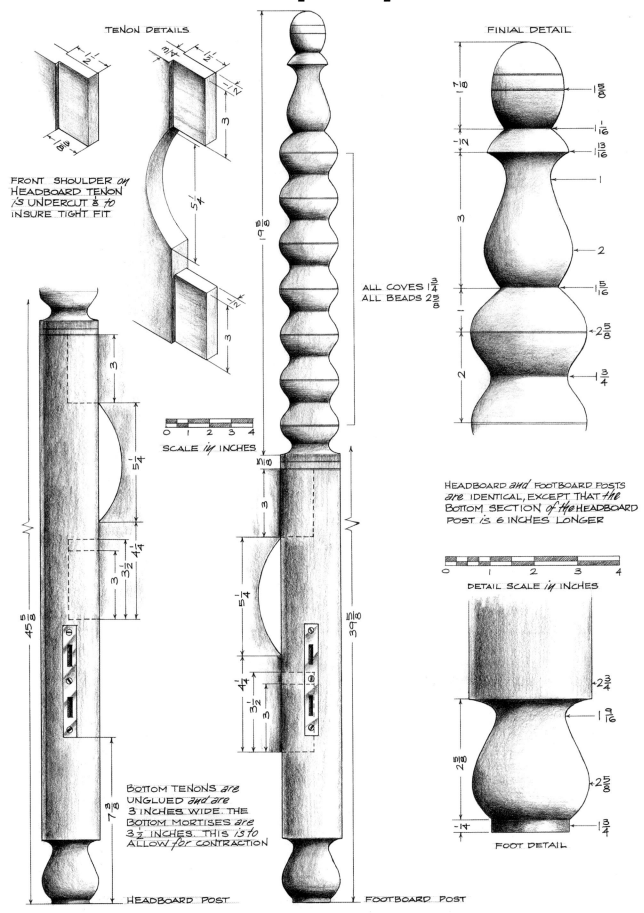

TENON DETAILS

FRONT SHOULDER *on* HEADBOARD TENON *is* UNDERCUT ⅛ *to* INSURE TIGHT FIT

SCALE *in* INCHES

ALL COVES 1¾
ALL BEADS 2⅝

FINIAL DETAIL

HEADBOARD *and* FOOTBOARD POSTS *are* IDENTICAL, EXCEPT THAT *the* BOTTOM SECTION *of the* HEADBOARD POST *is* 6 INCHES LONGER

DETAIL SCALE *in* INCHES

BOTTOM TENONS *are* UNGLUED *and are* 3 INCHES WIDE. THE BOTTOM MORTISES *are* 3½ INCHES. THIS *is to* ALLOW *for* CONTRACTION

HEADBOARD POST

FOOTBOARD POST

FOOT DETAIL

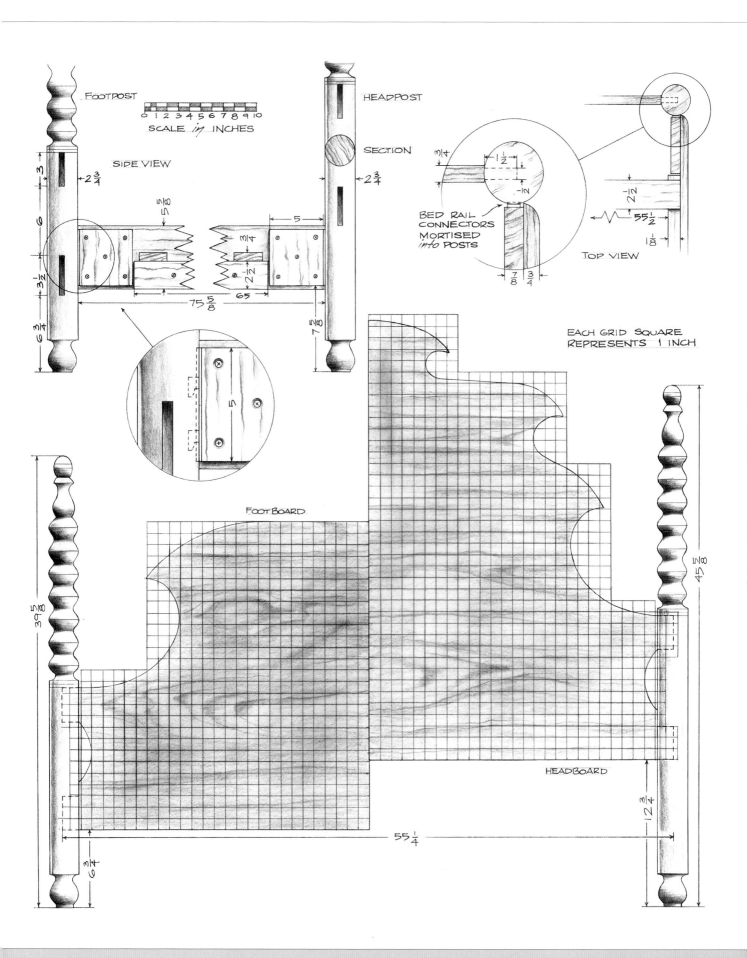

FOOTPOST

SCALE *in* INCHES

SIDE VIEW

HEADPOST

SECTION

BED RAIL
CONNECTORS
MORTISED
into POSTS

TOP VIEW

EACH GRID SQUARE
REPRESENTS 1 INCH

FOOTBOARD

HEADBOARD

CUTTING LIST ■ *pencil-post bed* inches (millimeters)

REFERENCE	QUANTITY	PART	STOCK	THICKNESS		WIDTH		LENGTH		COMMENTS
A	2	head posts	cherry	3	(76)	3	(76)	45⅝	(1159)	
B	2	foot posts	cherry	3	(76)	3	(76)	39⅝	(1006)	
C	1	headboard	cherry	¾	(19)	38½	(978)	55¼	(1403)	
D	1	footboard	cherry	¾	(19)	27	(686)	55¼	(1403)	
E	2	side rails	cherry	¾	(19)	5⅝	(143)	75⅝	(1921)	
F	2	side rail cleats	cherry	1⅛	(29)	2½	(64)	65⅛	(1654)	
G	4	screw blocks	cherry	⅞	(22)	5	(127)	5	(127)	
H	4	matress cleats	cherry	¾	(19)	2½	(64)	55½	(1410)	

hardware & supplies
- bed rail connectors (see supplier's page)
- No. 8 × 2" (50mm) coarse thread drywall or carcase screws

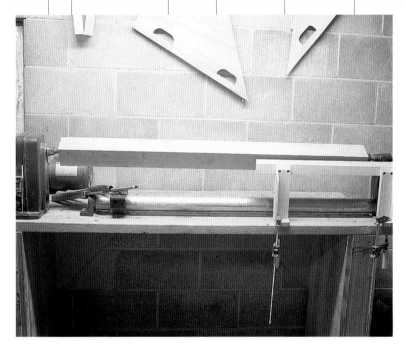

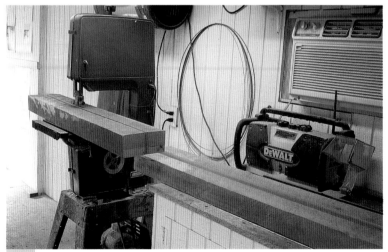

1 If your lathe is 36" (91cm) or less in length, here's an extension solution: I bought an extra mounting foot for my lathe's tubular bed and built a lathe stand that put the tail stock of my lathe almost 48" (122) from the head stock. I had to pull the bed tube from its mortise in the head stock assembly and mount the head stock end of the bed on the extra mounting foot. See photo.

2 Shop carefully for the 12/4 turning material for the legs. It must be good through and through because there is no back side on which you can hide a knot or a pitch pocket. Use a band saw to cut the leg stock to rough size.

3 Take the time to straighten the turning billets using a jointer, then run them through a thickness planer so the material is truly a square in cross section.

4 My turning kit is very simple. For these posts, I used only three tools: a 1⅛" (30mm) roughing gouge, a ⅜" (10mm) fingernail gouge, and a 1⅛" (30mm) skew.

5 Bring the heel of the bevel into the work, then raise the handle just a bit. In this position, the tool will cut without digging in.

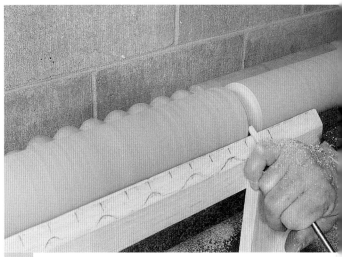

6 Because these turning blanks are thick, set the lathe on its slowest speed. Use a roughing gouge to convert the square blank into a cylinder. Remember to keep the rest no more than ⅜" (10mm) from the part being turned.

7 Because my tool rests are made of wood, I find it useful to mark off sections of the spindle on the rest. Then I can transfer the measurements directly from the rest to the work. When going from one blank to another, reposition the rest so the marks are correctly aligned for each new turning blank.

8 Basically these turnings are a series of alternating coves and beads.

9 With a roughing gouge, reduce the cylinder diameter to the thickest part of the vase, its pudgy little base. Then use a ³⁄₈" (10mm) fingernail gouge to create the cove below the vase and the more gradual cove at the vase's middle section.

10 The foot of each post is a cove above a big, fat bead which sits atop a little fillet. The fillet is formed with a paring chisel laid flat on the rest, bevel side down. Bring the chisel very carefully into the work; it will scrape out a smooth, flat surface.

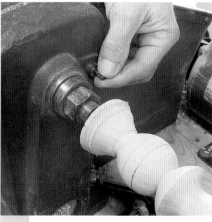

11 Lathe sanding goes quickly, particularly if high quality abrasives are used. Try experimenting with cloth-backed shop rolls. See suppliers page for a source.

12 My lathe has 36 holes near the circumference of its indexing head. These holes are spaced exactly 10° apart. This means that if I want to make two lines 90° apart on the outside diameter of a turned object, I simply count off nine holes on the indexing head.

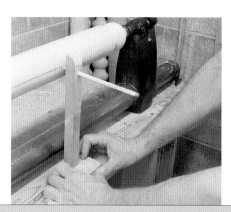

13 To draw the lines for the location of the mortises, make a jig that will slide along the bed of the lathe while holding a pencil. These lines need to be parallel with each post's axis of rotation and exactly 90° apart.

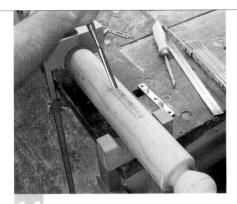

14 Using a paring chisel, remove enough material to mortise the female half of the bracket into place.

15 In order for the hooks on the male bracket to seat themselves properly, two secondary mortises must be cut inside the primary mortise. Use the female part to mark the widths of these secondary mortises.

16 To establish the lengths of the secondary mortises, vertically position the bracket where it will be when the hooks are fully engaged. Remember that the secondary mortises must be long enough to accept the hooks before they're fully seated as well as when they're fully seated.

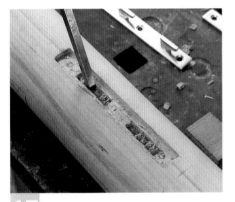

17 Although the width of these secondary mortises can be safely increased, the length can't be increased because there will be too little material left for the bracket mounting screws.

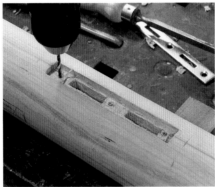

18 Drill the holes for the mounting screws. Use 2" (50mm) coarse-threaded drywall screws to mount the brackets.

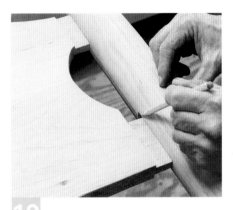

19 The headboard and footboard are attached to the posts with 1⅜" (35mm) tenons fit into mortises cut into the posts. To accommodate potential shrinkage, glue the top tenons on both the headboard and footboard. Leave the bottom tenons unglued. In addition, cut the mortise for the bottom tenon about ⅜" (10mm) longer than the tenon is wide. This will permit the headboard and footboard to shrink across their widths without cracking.

20 Although, at first glance, this may appear to be weak construction (because the headboard and footboard will have only one glued tenon on each end), this concept—the floating tenon—has a long history in cabinetmaking, and I know that if the joinery is well fit, there is no way for the combination of a glued and an unglued tenon to fail. A tightly fit mortise-and-tenon joint has significant mechanical strength—even unglued—and the glued upper tenon at each post will keep the post rigidly in position. Cut the mortises using a ⅜" (10mm) twist bit in a drill press, followed by a little cleaning with a ½" (13mm) paring chisel and a ¼" (6mm) mortise chisel.

21 It's important to match material for the head and foot boards. The worst of these I relegated to the headboard which will have one face against the wall. The boards that looked best on both sides, I set aside for the footboard. I then started shuffling material to match color and figure.

22 Edge-joint the selected boards. This can be done by hand using a long jointer plane or a stationary jointer. Clamp placement is important, particularly when the panel is as large as this one. Place the clamps alternately on the top and on the bottom with each clamp no more than 15" (380mm) from the next.

23 Unless a really colossal thickness planer is available, you'll have to surface these jumbo panels using hand tools. A hand held belt sander could be used, but it requires steady hands. That's why I switched to hand tools.

24 After the panels are surfaced, draw the pattern on the panel, and cut out the headboard and footboard using a saber saw.

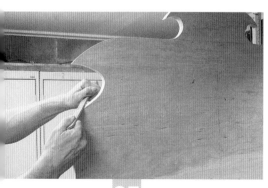

26 Cut the tenons that will fit into the mortises you cut in the posts. Cut them a little thick using a back saw. Cut the shoulders first, then the cheeks. You can also use a router to cut the tenons.

25 Finish the sawn edges with a plane, rasp and sandpaper.

27 Use a rabbet plane and to clean up the cheeks and bring the tenons to their final thicknesses.

28 The bed rails have rounded ends which echo the rounded shape of the posts against which they're fitted. These roundings can be cut using a hand plane.

For my finishing regimen, I sand each part with 150- and 220-grit sandpaper before assembling the piece. After assembly, I sand the piece with 220 grit, followed by a sanding with 320-grit sandpaper.

After the sanding, I apply the first coat of wipe-on finish (see supplier's page), without any concern for dripping. I then wipe it all off—or as much of it as I can wipe off—with soft rags (I prefer old T-shirts). The finish that remains has soaked into the surface of the wood.

The next day, the finish is dry and has raised the grain. I remove that raised grain with a thorough sanding of 320-grit sandpaper, followed by a sanding with 400-grit sandpaper.

I apply a second coat of wipe-on finish and once again wipe it with soft rags. This second wipe is critical. You must attempt to wipe off all the finish. Obviously you can't get everything. What you want is to leave behind a layer only a few molecules thick that will dry to a satiny smoothness. Anyplace covered with more than few molecule thick skin will dry roughened.

Finally, the next day, I resand with 1000-grit sandpaper and apply a coat of paste wax, which I buff thoroughly when dry.

29 The female halves of the brackets have already been mortised into the posts. The male halves need to be attached to the ends of the rails. It may be tempting to attach these brackets directly to the ends of the rails, but don't. Screws—and any other metal fasteners for that matter—have little holding power when driven into end grain. That's why the male brackets on my bed are fastened to mounting blocks which are screwed to the inside faces of the rails. I planed to thickness, ripped to width and cut to length the four mounting blocks. I then fastened the male brackets to the sides of the mounting blocks using 2" (50mm) drywall screws.

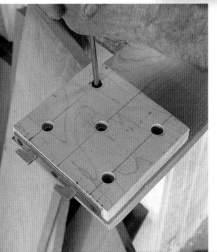

30 Predrill and countersink the holes for the mounting blocks, then attach them to the rails using five 1¼" (30mm) drywall screws.

entertainment

center

Entertainment centers were not a part of 18th-century homes. The need for a cupboard to house a television and stereo equipment did not exist. But utility cupboards occupied nearly every home, and excellent examples are available today.

This piece is one of those examples. The drawers set below the doors are a natural place to store DVDs or CDs. The doors open completely so there is open access to the electronic equipment, making it a perfect location for the television and you can add as many adjustable shelves as you need.

The construction also is easy to customize. Adding depth to the cabinet is simple and does not change the overall look. The frame-and-panel design lends itself to maintaining an antique look while accounting for panel movement from seasonal changes. This is one piece that you will enjoy building and living with while it holds today's most prominent household appliance.

by Glen Huey

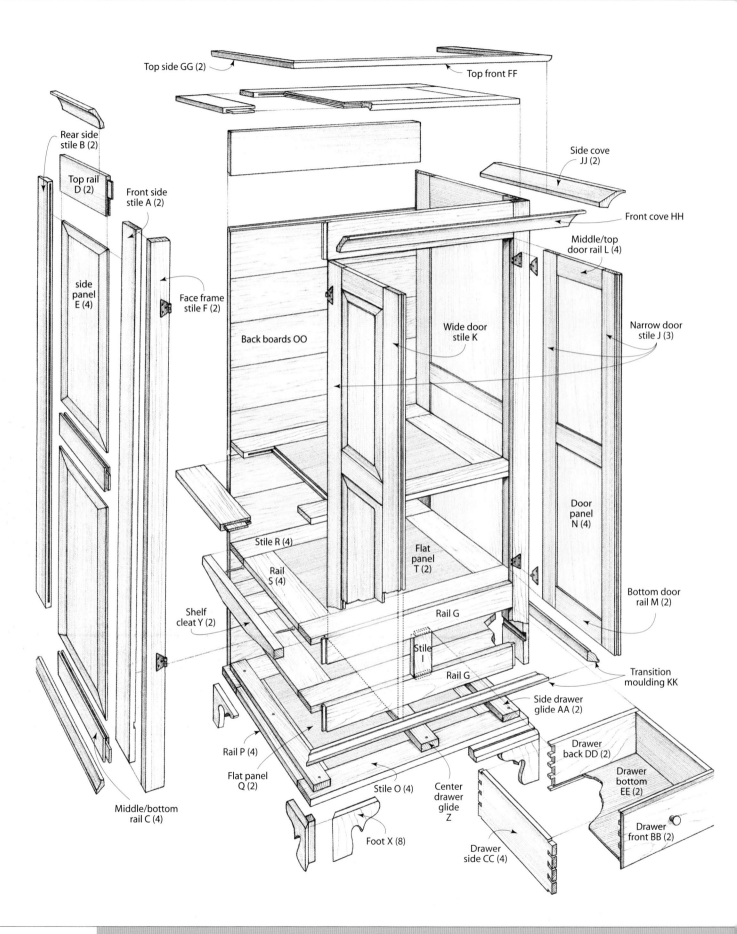

Top side GG (2)

Top front FF

Rear side
stile B (2)

Top rail
D (2)

Front side
stile A (2)

Side cove
JJ (2)

Front cove HH

Middle/top
door rail L (4)

side
panel
E (4)

Face frame
stile F (2)

Wide door
stile K

Narrow door
stile J (3)

Back boards OO

Door
panel
N (4)

Stile R (4)

Flat
panel
T (2)

Rail
S (4)

Shelf
cleat Y (2)

Rail G

Bottom door
rail M (2)

Stile
I

Rail G

Transition
moulding KK

Side drawer
glide AA (2)

Rail P (4)

Drawer
back DD (2)

Flat panel
Q (2)

Drawer
bottom
EE (2)

Stile O (4)

Center
drawer
glide
Z

Middle/bottom
rail C (4)

Foot X (8)

Drawer
front BB (2)

Drawer
side CC (4)

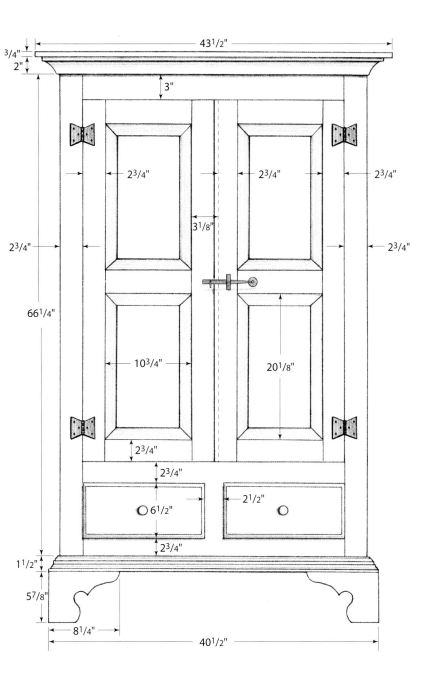

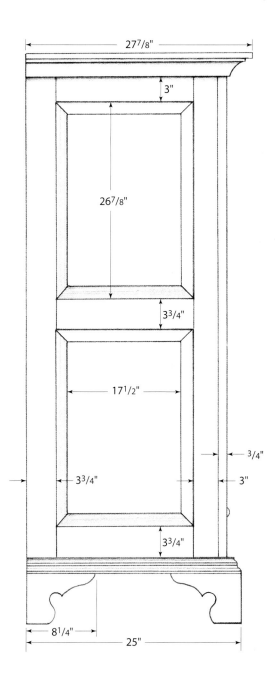

CUTTING LIST ■ *entertainment center* inches (millimeters)

REFERENCE	QUANTITY	PART	STOCK	THICKNESS		WIDTH		LENGTH		COMMENTS
A	2	front side stiles	poplar	$3/4$	(19)	3	(76)	$66^{1}/4$	(1683)	
B	2	rear side stiles	poplar	$3/4$	(19)	$3^{3}/4$	(95)	$66^{1}/4$	(1683)	
C	4	middle and bottom rails	poplar	$3/4$	(19)	$3^{3}/4$	(95)	20	(508)	$1^{1}/4$" (32mm) tenon both ends
D	2	top rails	poplar	$3/4$	(19)	5	(127)	20	(508)	$1^{1}/4$" (32mm) tenon both ends
E	4	raised cabinet panels	poplar	$5/8$	(16)	$18^{1}/8$	(460)	$27^{1}/2$	(699)	
F	2	face-frame stiles	poplar	$3/4$	(19)	$2^{3}/4$	(70)	$66^{1}/4$	(1683)	
G	2	face-frame rails	poplar	$3/4$	(19)	$2^{3}/4$	(70)	35	(889)	$1^{1}/4$" (32mm) tenon both ends
H	1	face-top rail	poplar	$3/4$	(19)	5	(127)	35	(889)	$1^{1}/4$" (32mm) tenon both ends
I	1	drawer divider	poplar	$3/4$	(19)	$2^{1}/2$	(64)	9	(229)	$1^{1}/4$" (32mm) tenon both ends
J	3	narrow door stiles	poplar	$3/4$	(19)	$2^{3}/4$	(70)	$49^{1}/4$	(1251)	
K	1	wide door stile	poplar	$3/4$	(19)	$3^{1}/8$	(79)	$49^{1}/4$	(1251)	
L	4	middle and top door rails	poplar	$3/4$	(19)	$2^{3}/4$	(70)	$13^{1}/4$	(337)	$1^{1}/4$" (32mm) tenon both ends
M	2	bottom door rails	poplar	$3/4$	(19)	$3^{1}/2$	(89)	$13^{1}/4$	(337)	$1^{1}/4$" (32mm) tenon both ends
N	2	raised door panels	poplar	$5/8$	(16)	$11^{3}/8$	(289)	$20^{3}/4$	(527)	

Case top and bottom panels

REFERENCE	QUANTITY	PART	STOCK	THICKNESS		WIDTH		LENGTH		COMMENTS
O	4	stiles	poplar	$3/4$	(19)	3	(76)	37	(940)	
P	4	rails	poplar	$3/4$	(19)	5	(127)	20	(508)	$1^{1}/4$" (32mm) tenon both ends
Q	2	flat panels	poplar	$3/4$	(19)	$18^{1}/8$	(460)	$27^{5}/8$	(702)	

Shelves

REFERENCE	QUANTITY	PART	STOCK	THICKNESS		WIDTH		LENGTH		COMMENTS
R	4	stiles	poplar	$3/4$	(19)	3	(76)	$36^{3}/8$	(924)	
S	4	rails	poplar	$3/4$	(19)	5	(127)	19	(483)	$1^{1}/4$" (32mm) tenon both ends
T	2	flat panels	poplar	$3/4$	(19)	$17^{1}/8$	(435)	27	(686)	
U	1	base-frame front	poplar	$3/4$	(19)	3	(76)	$40^{1}/4$	(1022)	miter cut both ends
V	2	base-frame sides	poplar	$3/4$	(19)	3	(76)	$26^{1}/8$	(664)	miter cut one end
W	1	base-frame back	poplar	$3/4$	(19)	3	(76)	$36^{3}/4$	(933)	$1^{1}/4$" (32mm) tenon both ends
X	8	feet	poplar	$3/4$	(19)	$5^{7}/8$	(149)	$8^{1}/4$	(210)	6 cut to pattern
Y	2	shelf cleats	poplar	$3/4$	(19)	2	(51)	23	(584)	
Z	1	center drawer glide	poplar	$3/4$	(19)	$2^{1}/2$	(64)	23	(584)	
AA	2	outside drawer glides	poplar	$3/4$	(19)	1	(25)	23	(584)	
BB	2	drawer fronts	poplar	$3/4$	(19)	$6^{3}/4$	(171)	$15^{5}/8$	(397)	
CC	4	drawer sides	poplar	$1/2$	(13)	$6^{3}/8$	(162)	20	(508)	
DD	2	drawer backs	poplar	$1/2$	(13)	$5^{5}/8$	(143)	$14^{7}/8$	(378)	
EE	2	drawer bottoms	poplar	$5/8$	(16)	20	(508)	15	(381)	cut to fit

Mouldings

REFERENCE	QUANTITY	PART	STOCK	THICKNESS		WIDTH		LENGTH		COMMENTS
FF	1	top front	poplar	$3/4$	(19)	$3^{3}/4$	(95)	$43^{1}/2$	(1105)	miter cut both ends
GG	2	top sides	poplar	$3/4$	(19)	$3^{3}/4$	(95)	$27^{7}/8$	(708)	miter cut one end
HH	1	front cove	poplar	$3/4$	(19)	3	(76)	44	(1118)	miter cut both ends
JJ	2	side coves	poplar	$3/4$	(19)	3	(76)	29	(737)	miter cut one end
KK	2	transition	poplar	$3/4$	(19)	$1^{1}/2$	(38)	52	(1320)	makes 2 pieces
LL	1	interior door catch	poplar	$5/8$	(16)	$3/4$	(19)	$2^{1}/2$	(64)	
MM	1	top door stop	poplar	$5/8$	(16)	$2^{3}/4$	(70)	$3^{1}/2$	(89)	
NN	1	bottom door stop	poplar	$3/4$	(19)	$3/4$	(19)	$2^{3}/4$	(70)	
OO		back boards	poplar	$5/8$	(16)	65	(1651)	$37^{1}/2$	(953)	random width boards

hardware & supplies

- 4—$2^{1}/2$" (65mm) × 3"(75mm) door hinges, black iron
- 1—door catch, black iron
- 2—$1^{1}/8$" (30mm) door knobs, black iron
- nails, clout or shingle

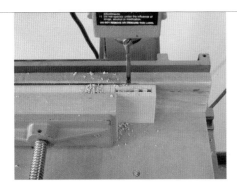

1 The case sides are made with a series of mortise and tenons that are fitted with raised panels. Lay out the mortise locations on the stiles of the case sides cut to size from the cutting list. Create the $\frac{1}{4}$" × 3" × $1\frac{1}{4}$" (6mm × 76mm × 32mm) slots for the middle and bottom rail tenons as well as the $\frac{1}{4}$" × $4\frac{1}{4}$" × $1\frac{1}{4}$" (6mm × 108mm × 32mm) slots for the top rail tenons. Use the step method of cutting the mortises. Cut every other $\frac{1}{4}$" (6mm)× $\frac{1}{4}$" (6mm) hole from end to end on your mortise, then return to remove the balance of the material on a second pass. This keeps equal pressure on all sides of the mortising chisel and bit sets and reduces undo ware.

a b

c d

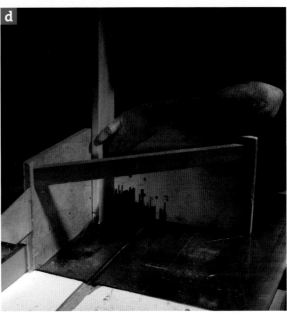

2 Here's how to make the tenons using the table saw: Set the blade to $\frac{1}{4}$" (6mm) in height and the fence at $1\frac{1}{4}$" (32mm) (this includes the width of the blade). Make a cut on each flat side of all rails for the two sides (Photo a). Then raise the blade height to $\frac{3}{8}$" (10mm) and don't change the fence setting. Cut one edge on the top and bottom rails and both edges of the middle rails (Photo b). Next, move the fence $\frac{3}{8}$" towards the blade and cut the uncut edges (Photo c). (This creates the haunch area that fills the groove for the panels.) Use a tenoning fixture to cut the tenons to fit into the mortises (Photo d). Cut equal amounts from each face to center the tenon on the rails.

3 Cut the tenons to width using the band saw. Note the haunch at the top of the tenon.

4 Use the table saw to cut the groove for the raised panels. Set the height to $3/8$" (10mm). (This matches the haunched portion of the tenon.) Set the fence at a $1/4$" (6mm). Make a pass along each piece of the frame, reverse the pieces, make a second pass, cutting the groove at $1/4$" (6mm) wide. This will center the groove in the rails and stiles. Fine-tune this cut, if necessary, so the tenons fit into the grooves. The inset shows the completed mortise-and-tenon joint. The haunch will fit into the groove, filling in any opening.

5 Mill the cabinet panels to thickness. Dry fit a side frame. Measure the inside width and height of the panel openings and add $5/8$" (16mm) to each dimension. Tilt the table saw blade to 12°, set the fence at $3/16$" (5mm) from the blade at its lowest point (flush with the tabletop) and raise the blade just high enough to make the cut. I recommend using an extended fence for this procedure. It allows you to clamp the panel to the fence to hold it steady. Cut all four edges of the panel.

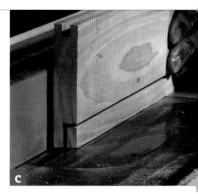

6 To cut the rabbet on the inside rear edge of the rear side stiles, set the saw blade height to $^7/_{16}$" (11mm) and the fence to $^3/_4$" (19mm) (including the blade's width). Make the cut. Now set the blade height to $^3/_4$" (19mm) and the fence so the rabbet is $^7/_{16}$" (11mm). (The fence setting at this stage will depend on the thickness of the material.)

7 Sand the panels with 180-grit sandpaper, add glue into the mortises and on each tenon and assemble the case sides. Then fit the joints together for one half of the frames. Slide the panels into the groove and slip the balance of the frame together. Add clamps to complete the first side. Repeat the steps for the second side and allow the glue to dry.

8 Mill the parts for the face frame to size according to the cutting list and cut the mortises in the top, middle and bottom rails. You also need to cut a mortise in the bottom and middle rails for the drawer divider. Next, cut the tenons on the rails and the drawer divider as you did in step 2. This time the blade height is set at $^1/_4$" (6mm). Make cuts on all four sides of each rail. Then use the tenoning fixture to cut the tenons to thickness and width. With the joints cut and fit, assemble the face frame as shown.

8

9 The top and bottom panels as well as the shelves are more lessons in mortise-and-tenon joinery. You will create the mortises, tenons and grooves just as you did for the cabinet sides. However, instead of a raised panel, these parts have flat panels. They are made by cutting a rabbet (as shown in step 8) on both sides of the flat panel. The resulting tongue is 1/4" (6mm) thick and 1/4" (6mm) long. Assemble the parts using glue only at the frame's joints.

10 Cut a groove for the top and bottom panels. Use a straightedge and a 3/4" (19mm) pattern bit to cut the grooves. The groove for the top panel is 1" (25mm) down from the top edge of the case. The bottom panel is flush with the top edge of the bottom face-frame rail. Install the panels in the grooves and attach with No.8 × 1 1/4" (30mm) screws.

11 Lay the cabinet on its back and position the face frame on the cabinet. Using glue and clamps, attach the face frame to the cabinet.

12 When the glue has dried, use a router with a bottom-mount bearing to trim the face frame flush to the side of the cabinet.

13 The shelf cleats are attached to the cabinet's side stiles with No.8 × 1 1/4" (30mm) screws. Locate the cleats so the shelf rests 1/4" (6mm) above the middle rail of the face frame. The shelf will act as a stop for the doors.

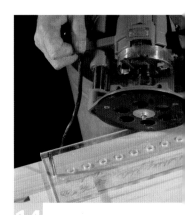

14 Using a homemade template, rout the holes for the shelf pins. Be sure to locate the template at the same height for each set of holes. This step will assures the shelves are both level and secure.

15 Install the drawer glides to the cabinet bottom. Attach the two side glides using brads and glue. The center glide is attached with screws to the front and rear stiles of the bottom panel.

16 Slide one of the shelves onto the shelf cleats and hold it tight to the case front as you attach it to the cleat using screws.

17 Sand the cabinet. This is to be a painted piece so there is no need to go beyond 150-grit sandpaper.

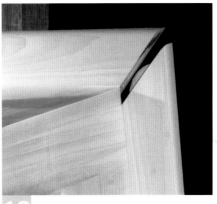

18 To make the top mouldings, use a ¹⁄₂" (13mm) roundover bit to rout a bullnose on one edge of the moulding. The moulding overhangs the cabinet ³⁄₄" (19mm) and is attached to the top of the cabinet using screws. Glue and biscuits keep the mitered corners tight.

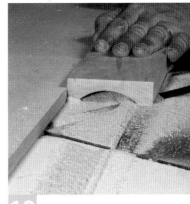

19 To make the cove moulding, attach an auxiliary fence to the table saw top at an angle to the blade. Make ¹⁄₁₆" (2mm) cuts on each pass. Raise the blade until you reach the desired depth of cut.

20 To complete the cove moulding, set the blade to 45° and make the two longer cuts with the stock face up and flat on the tabletop. To make the smaller cuts, set the blade to 90°. Place the long cut edge against the fence to complete the moulding.

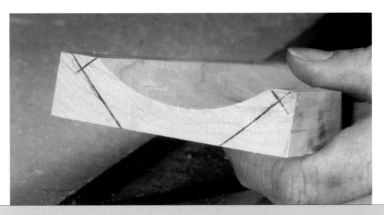

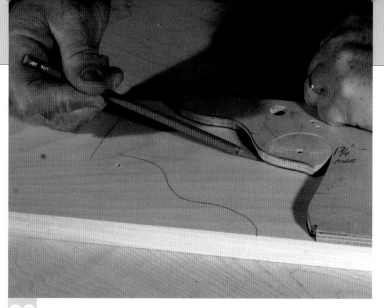

21 Cut the corners of the cove moulding at 45° and fit them to the case. Attach the moulding using brads at both the top and bottom edges of the cove.

22 Cut the blanks for the feet. Make the pattern of ¼" (6mm)-thick plywood. Trace the profile on six of the foot blanks. Mark the center point of the drilled area.

23 Use a 1¾" (45mm) Forstner bit to cut holes in the feet. These holes will form the spur of the foot.

24 Cut the profiles using a band saw, then sand the edges smooth.

25 Cut the miters on the two right-handed feet.

26 Reverse the miter gauge and cut the two left-handed feet as shown. For safety reasons, do not try to cut the left feet using the set up in step 25.

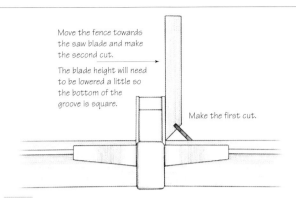

Move the fence towards the saw blade and make the second cut.

The blade height will need to be lowered a little so the bottom of the groove is square.

Make the first cut.

27 Cut a slot for splines into each of the mitered feet. Keep the blade at the 45° angle. Change the height of the blade and reposition the fence to cut the slot. Make two passes on each foot to create the $\frac{1}{4}$" (6mm) slot. As you adjust the fence for the second cut, it's necessary to adjust the height of the blade. If the fence is moved toward the blade, the height will decrease. The opposite is true if you move away from the blade. See the illustration for details.

28 Add glue to the slots and the face of the miter cuts. Insert the plywood spline and assemble the foot. I like to wrap the assembly with duct tape to hold it until the glue dries.

29 In the back edge of the two profiled feet, cut a rabbet that will accept the unprofiled foot. Then make a 45° cut on the unprofiled foot.

30 Glue and screw the back foot assemblies together.

31 Cut the parts for the base frame. Miter the front corners and make a mortise-and-tenon joint for the intersection of the back and sides. Use a biscuit joiner to cut a slot for No.20 biscuits in the mitered cuts.

32 Assemble the mortise-and-tenon joints first, then add glue for the biscuits. Make sure the clamps from front to back are centered on the mortise-and-tenon joint. Apply even pressure to all four clamps. Check the assembly for squareness.

33 Attach the foot assemblies to the frame using glue, and hold the foot in place with a clamp. Then, using glue and brads, install the glue blocks. The glue blocks add tremendous strength to the foot assemblies.

35 Lay the cabinet on its back and position the base on the cabinet. Countersink the holes drilled in step 34. Then, using No.8 × 1¼" (30mm) screws, attach the base to the cabinet.

34 To complete the base assembly, rout a profile on the edges of the sides and front of the frame's edges. Then, sand the entire base. Next, position the cabinet on the frame and draw the outline of the outside of the cabinet on it. To mark where the screws can be installed when the base is attached to the cabinet, predrill ⅜" (9mm) holes inside the line.

36 Rout the profile of the transition moulding on double-wide stock, then rip the stock to the final width of the moulding.

37 The transition moulding covers the joint of the base frame and the cabinet. It has a 45° mitered connection at the front corners. The back is cut flush with the rear edge of the cabinet's back. Attach the moulding using glue and brads.

39 This photo shows the lap joint at the center stiles of the doors. The left door is latched, so its center stile needs a rabbet in order for the operable door to overlap it when the doors are closed. (The overlap is ³⁄₈" [9mm].) The latched door will be rabbeted on the face side and the other door on the back side.

40 Cut the dovetail joinery in the drawer backs and sides. See chapter 9, steps 15-23 for instructions for cutting dovetails in the drawer backs and sides. The lipped drawer fronts are joined to the sides with half-blind dovetails. After cutting the ³⁄₈" × ½" (9mm × 13mm) rabbet on the top and side edges of the drawer fronts, scribe a line that is equal to the thickness of the sides on the inside of the drawer fronts.

38 The doors are assembled using mortise-and-tenon joinery and raised panels like the cabinet sides. Decide whether the right or left door will be operable and which will be latched. The latched door will need the wider door stile (in the center of the door). I made the right-hand door operable. I positioned the wider stile on the right-hand side of the left door.

cutting the dovetail sockets

■ **define the dovetails (a)**

Layout the dovetails (I use a 12° angle) on the ends of the fronts and extend the lines about 1½" (38mm) towards the center of the fronts. These are the lines you cut to define the edges of the dovetail sockets. Be careful not to nick the drawer lip. Cut down the lines as far as possible. This will mean less to clear with the chisels.

■ **removing material (b)**

Visable overcut from the saw is acceptable and seen in any number of museum collections of furniture. Place the chisel in front of the scribed line and set the cut. As you hit the chisel, it will move toward the line. Set the cut across each of the sockets. Then remove the waste material with a chisel. The corners of the pins (the remaining material after the socket is created) are fragile and easily knocked off. To remove the waste, take small bites starting at the corners of the socket. Keep the chisel at a 45° angle to remove each corner as shown, then remove the middle area of the socket.

■ **depth of sockets (c)**

Repeat these steps of removing the waste until the bottom of the socket is set. It should be flush with the lip of the drawer.

■ **width of sockets (d)**

Use a ½" (13mm) chisel to pare down the sides of the sockets to the layout lines. This will become the pattern for the dovetails that fit these sockets, i.e., the look of the completed dovetail joint for the drawer. Make them look great!

■ **back of sockets (e)**

Use a ¼" (6mm) chisel to trim the back corners of the sockets. Make sure that the back wall of the socket angles away from the edge at a 2° slope. This will help to close the joint when it is assembled.

■ **finished sockets**

When the dovetail sockets are completed, the drawer front is set onto the scribed drawer sides and the socket layout is transferred to the sides. Cut the tails.

finished dovetail sockets

a b

c d

e

43 The beginning of the finishing process is to apply a coat of water-based aniline dye, lightly sand with 400-grit paper to smooth the raised grain and apply two coats of shellac. There are two reasons for doing this. One, it seals the wood to allow better manipulation of the paint and, two, it provides a finish for the interior of the piece. I use an acrylic latex paint. Before applying the paint, give it texture by adding fine sawdust.

42 Complete the drawers by cutting the groove in the bottoms and installing them using a square nail.

44 Work a small area at a time. Here, I'm working on one of the doors. Apply the paint to the surface and allow it to dry a bit. The direction of the paint strokes will show on the finished project so I like to paint in the direction of the wood grain.

45 Once the paint has dried a little, use a clean wet rag to simulate worn areas (rub the surface to let the stain show in some places). The sawdust helps the rag grab the paint. Be careful because a little aging goes a long way.

46 If you find that you have overdone the "aging" a bit, one of the great things about this process is that you can add more paint.

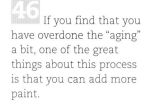

47 This photo shows how the saw-dust creeps into corners and builds up to simulate aging. I chose hand-hammered black iron for hardware. The butterfly hinges are a great period look, as is the latch. Once the doors are hung, you need to add the door stops and the catch. The catch is a piece of wood that is screwed to inside of the door and swivels to catch the face frame when the door is closed.

48 The backboards have shiplap joinery. There is no finish on these pieces, so as they age, they get their own patina. The boards run horizontally and are nailed to the case sides. Gapping between them depends on the time of year the cabinet is built because they will expand and contract with seasonal changes. Each board has one nail per case side, but the top and bottom boards have two nails per side.

49 A protective coat or two of paste wax can add a sheen to the painted finish.

three-drawer *dresser* 9

This piece is simple in construction but excels in features. It boasts fluted columns, beaded drawers and two small drawers on top. The finished piece is worthy of a look by anyone who views it.

You can customize this design to suit your needs—perhaps adding another dresser drawer or two. As it is shown with the two top drawers installed, it makes a perfect dresser with ample storage for clothing, watches, jewelry and such.

by Dave Griessmann

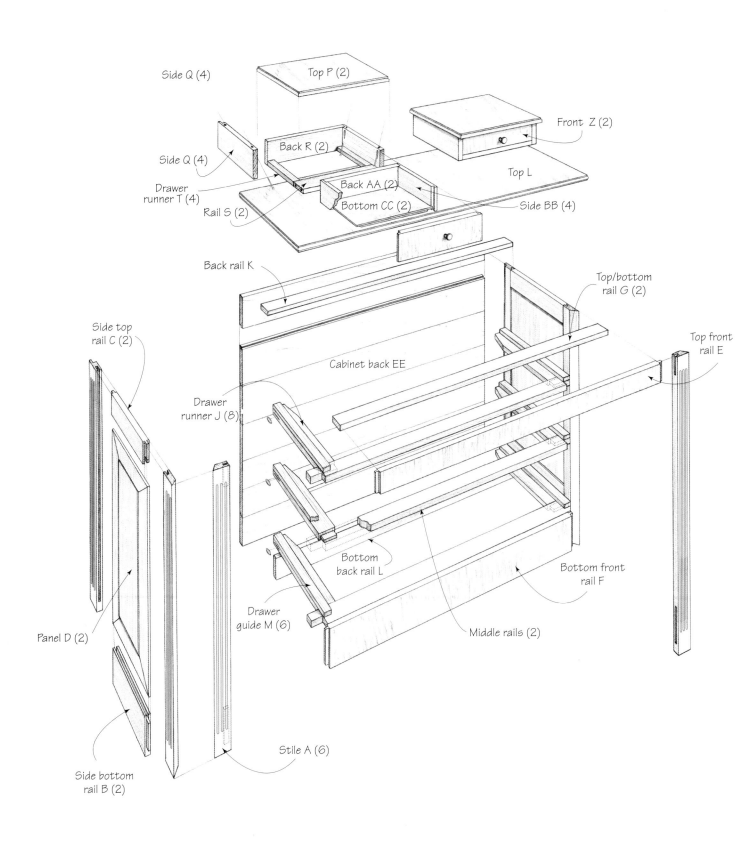

Side Q (4)

Top P (2)

Side Q (4)

Front Z (2)

Back R (2)

Drawer
runner T (4)

Back AA (2)

Top L

Rail S (2)

Bottom CC (2)

Side BB (4)

Back rail K

Top/bottom
rail G (2)

Side top
rail C (2)

Cabinet back EE

Top front
rail E

Drawer
runner J (8)

Panel D (2)

Drawer
guide M (6)

Bottom
back rail L

Bottom front
rail F

Middle rails (2)

Stile A (6)

Side bottom
rail B (2)

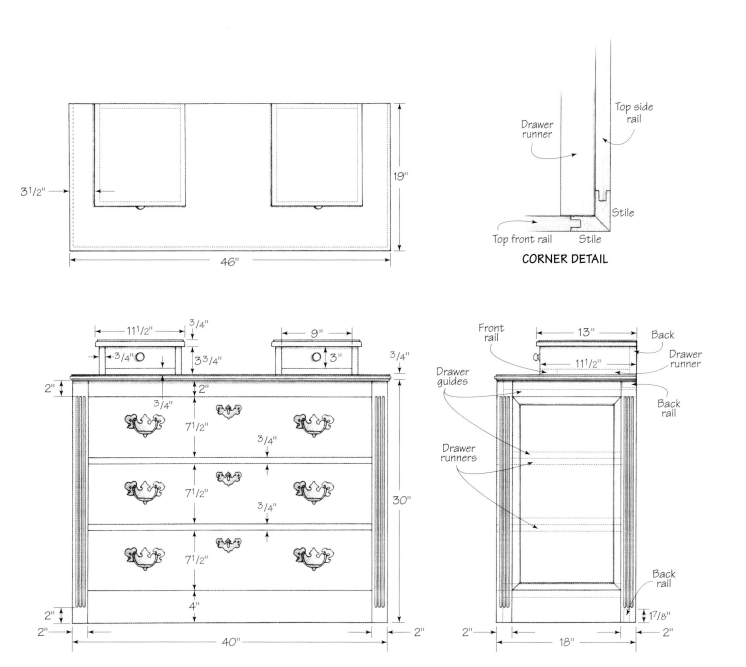

CORNER DETAIL

Drawer runner

Top side rail

Stile

Top front rail

Stile

19"

3¹/₂"

46"

11¹/₂"

3/4"

3/4"

3³/₄"

9"

3"

3/4"

2"

2"

3/4"

7¹/₂"

3/4"

7¹/₂"

3/4"

7¹/₂"

4"

30"

2"

2"

2"

40"

2"

Front rail

13"

Back

Drawer runner

11¹/₂"

Drawer guides

Back rail

Drawer runners

Back rail

1⁷/₈"

2"

18"

2"

CUTTING LIST ■ *three-drawer dresser* inches (millimeters)

REFERENCE	QUANTITY	PART	STOCK	THICKNESS		WIDTH		LENGTH		COMMENTS
Bottom cabinet										
A	6	stiles	maple	¾	(19)	2	(51)	30	(762)	2 w/ ⁷⁄₁₆" (11mm) × ¾" (19mm) ra
B	2	side bottom rails	maple	¾	(19)	4½	(115)	16½	(419)	1" (25mm) tenon both ends
C	2	side top rails	maple	¾	(19)	3⅝	(92)	16½	(419)	1"(25mm) tenon both ends
D	2	panels	maple	½	(13)	14¾	(375)	25	(635)	
E	1	top front rail	maple	¾	(19)	2	(51)	42	(1067)	1"(25mm) tenon both ends
F	1	bottom front rail	maple	¾	(19)	4	(102)	42	(1067)	1"(25mm) tenon both ends
G	2	top and bottom rails	maple	¾	(19)	2¾	(70)	42⁷⁄₁₆	(1078)	
H	2	middle rails	maple	¾	(19)	2	(51)	42⁷⁄₁₆	(1078)	¾" (19mm) × 1¼" (32mm) notch
J	8	drawer runners	poplar	¾	(19)	3	(76)	15¾	(400)	½" (13mm) tenon one end
K	2	back rails	poplar	¾	(19)	1⅞	(48)	42½	(1080)	
L	1	top	maple	¾	(19)	19	(483)	46	(1168)	³⁄₁₆" (5mm) roundover top edges, ⅜" (10mm) roundover bottom ed
M	6	drawer guides	poplar	½	(13)	1¼	(32)	14	(356)	
N	6	drawer stops	poplar	½	(13)	¾	(19)	¾	(19)	
Top cases										
P	2	tops	maple	¾	(19)	11½	(292)	13	(330)	³⁄₁₆" (5mm) roundover edges
Q	4	sides	maple	¾	(19)	3¾	(96)	11½	(292)	⅜" (10mm) × ¾" (19mm) rabbet
R	2	backs	maple	¾	(19)	3¾	(96)	10	(254)	
S	2	rail	maple	¾	(19)	3	(76)	9	(229)	
T	4	drawer runners	maple	¾	(19)	¾	(19)	8¼	(210)	
U	2	drawer stops	maple	¾	(19)	¾	(19)	3	(76)	
Lower drawers										
V	3	fronts	maple	¾	(19)	7½	(191)	39¹⁵⁄₁₆	(1014)	¼" (6mm) × ¼" (6mm) groove
W	3	backs	poplar	½	(13)	7⁹⁄₁₆	(192)	39¹⁵⁄₁₆	(1014)	¼" (6mm) × ¼" (6mm) groove
X	6	sides	poplar	½	(13)	7⁹⁄₁₆	(192)	16	(406)	¼ "(6mm) × ¼" (6mm) groove
Y	3	bottoms	poplar	⅝	(16)	16	(406)	40	(1016)	bevel edges to ¼" (6mm)
Upper drawers										
Z	2	fronts	maple	¾	(19)	3	(76)	9	(229)	¼" (6mm) × ¼" (6mm) groove
AA	2	backs	poplar	½	(13)	3	(76)	9	(229)	¼" (6mm) × ¼" (6mm) groove
BB	4	sides	poplar	½	(13)	3	(76)	10½	(267)	¼" (6mm) × ¼" (6mm) groove
CC	2	bottoms	poplar	¼	(6)	8¾	(222)	11	(279)	flat panel
DD		drawer front beading	maple	³⁄₁₆	(5)	¾	(19)	30 ft	(9m)	cut to lengths as needed
EE		cabinet back	poplar	⅝	(16)	43⅛	(1095)	30	(762)	random width boards with half-lap joints

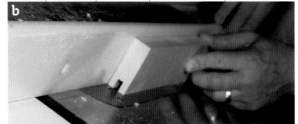

hardware & supplies
- ¼" (6mm) silicone bronze carriage bolts
- No. 8 × 1¼" (30mm) silicone bronze flathead screws

1 Mill the six stiles. Then, at the table saw, set your blade height to ⅜" (10mm) and fence to ¼" (6mm) away from the blade. Cut a groove along each stile and turn each stile around to cut the other side so you have a ⅜" (10mm) × ¼" (6mm) groove on center.

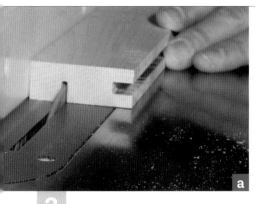
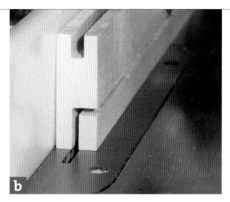

2 Cut a $^{7}/_{16}$" (11mm) × $^{3}/_{4}$" (6mm) rabbet (to receive the backboards) on the back two stiles. On the remaining four stiles, match up two stile sets to make each front corner and cut a 45° angle from the outside face coming into the case.

3 Set up a $^{3}/_{8}$" (9mm) roundover bit in your router table to make a shallow groove. Then, use it to make the three flutes in the stiles. On the fence, mark two start/stop lines 2" (51mm) from both the leading and trailing sides of your router bit on your fence. Next, mark the center of the stiles and plunge cut each stile 2" (51mm) from the top of the stile. Stop 2" from the bottom of the stile. Now, on both sides, rout a groove centered between the center flute and the edge of the stile.

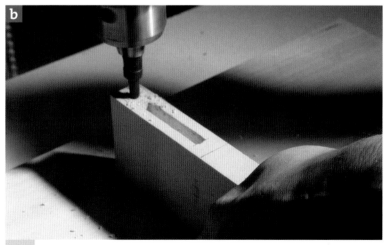

4 Mill the front and side rails of the case, all drawer dividers, drawer runners and the back rail supports to the sizes on the cutting list. Then mark the locations for the mortises on the stiles. Also mark the locations for the mortises and screw locations on the drawer dividers. Cut the mortises, predrill the holes and notch the two middle drawer dividers.

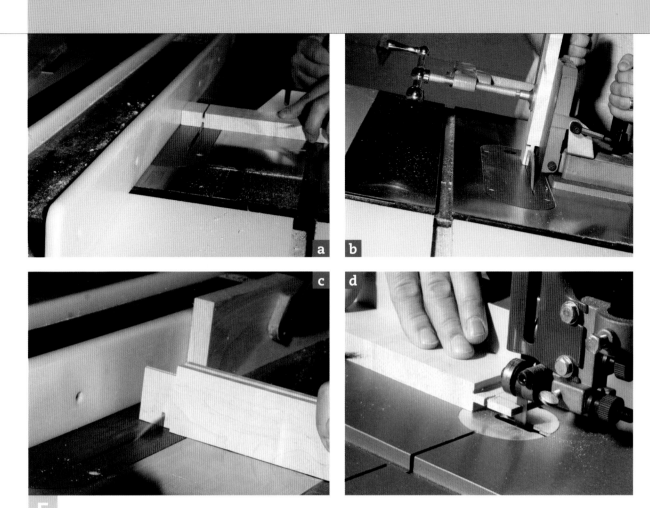

5 Set the table saw blade height to $1/4$" (6mm) and the fence to $7/8$" (22mm). Cut the tenon's shoulders on the top, bottom and one side of the rails, and all four sides of the drawer runners (Photo a). Now set the blade height to 1" (25mm) and use a tenoning fixture to cut both sides of the tenons on each end of the rails and drawer runners (Photo b). Clamp a $3/4$" (19mm)-thick start block to the fence, set the blade height to $3/8$" (9mm) and, measuring from the start block, set the fence at $1\frac{1}{4}$" (32mm). Using a miter gauge, set the end of the tenon against the start block and make the first cut of the tenon's haunch on both ends of rails (Photo c). Finally, set the fence on your band saw $3/8$" (9mm) from the blade and the second cut to create the haunch.

6 Lay two corner stiles face up on a flat surface. Butt the beveled edges together and use duct tape to hold the pieces in place. Flip over the assembly and brush glue in the beveled joint. Then fold the two pieces together to form a 90° angle. Let the glue dry.

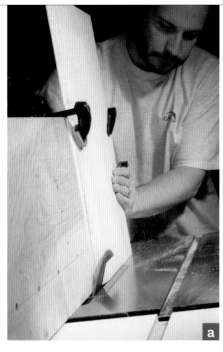

7 Cut the side panel blanks to size as shown on the cutting list. A plywood fence extension slides over my table saw fence to hold large panels vertical. Tilt the saw blade to 12° and set the fence to approximately ³⁄₁₆" (5mm) from the blade. Clamp the panel to the extension and cut bevels on all four edges of the panel. Check the fit of the bevel in the stile and rail grooves. The panel needs to fit into the groove about ¹⁄₄" (6mm).

8 It's time to glue up and assemble the side assemblies. Set a front stile assembly on edge, add glue to the ends of a top and bottom rail and put them in place on the stile. Slide the panel in place and put the a back stile in place. On a flat surface, clamp the assembly across the frame joints until the glue dries.

9 Place both side assemblies on their front faces and glue the top and bottom front rails in place. Then, using screws and glue, install the drawer rails as shown.

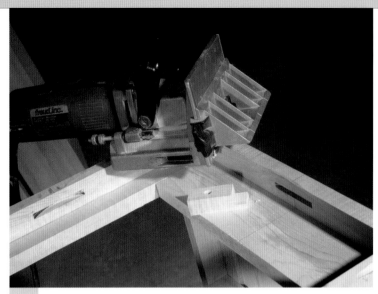

10 Using a pocket-hole jig, drill a hole in the nontenoned end of each bottom-case drawer runner. Apply glue to the tenons and insert them into the drawer rails. Use a pocket screw to attach the rail to the back stile.

11 Attach the back rail using glue and pocket-hole screws. Use a biscuit joiner to cut double-wide slots on the inside of the case rails. The top of the slot is ¼" (6mm) from the top of the cabinet. Make the first cut, then lower the cutter ⅛" (2mm) and make the second cut. This should create a ¼" (6mm)-wide slots for the wooden clips.

13 Flip over the top, set the case upside down on it and use No. 8 × 1¼" (30mm) wood screws to attach the clips. They hold the top tightly to the cabinet but allow for seasonal movement.

12 Attach the drawer guides to the drawer runners using a bead of glue and brads. Then rout a ³⁄₁₆" (5mm) roundover on the top edges of the top and a ⅜" (9mm) roundover on the bottom of the edges.

14 Cut the parts of the upper cases. Rout a ⅜" (9mm) roundover on both the top and bottom edges of the top. Using the bottom rails as spacers, attach the sides to the top using pocket screws. Then attach the bottom rail and back to the sides. Use glue and brads to install the drawer runners.

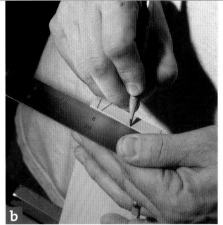

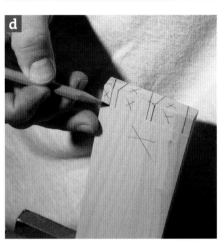

15 Cut all the drawer parts to size as shown in the cutting list. Mark the outside face and top edges on all the drawer parts. Use a scribe to mark the thickness of the sides onto the drawer back (Photo a). Use a 12° dovetail-marking gauge or a sliding T-bevel to lay out the pins (Photos b-d).

16 Using a 12° platform on your band saw, roughcut the pins and finish them at the bench with your chisels.

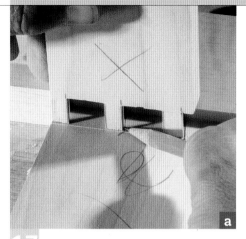
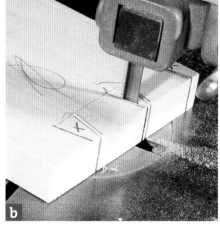

17 On the drawer back, transfer/scribe the pin locations from the ends of the sides. Remove the waste using a band saw and chisels.

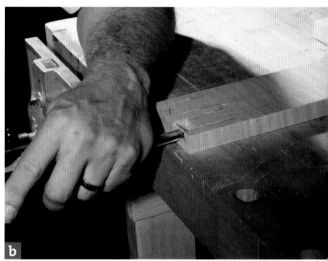

18 Scribe the location of the dovetail pins on the drawer fronts, scribe the length of the pins on the ends and cut the tails. Use a handsaw to cut on the waste side of the pin lines. Cut down to the scribe mark on the ends of the drawer front. The saw cut will extend into the inside of the drawer front. That's OK. The cuts add to the handmade look. Use chisels to remove the waste.

19 Install a ¼" (6mm) straight-cut bit into your router table. Set the height of the bit to ¼" (6mm) above the tabletop and set the fence so there's ¾" (19mm) between it and the bit. Cut the groove on the inside face of the drawer sides and drawer front.

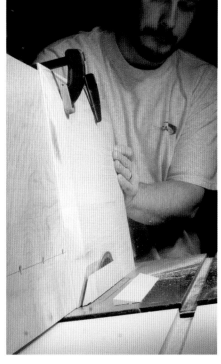

21 Double-check the measurements for the drawer bottoms and cut them to size. Use the extended fence to cut the 12° bevels on the sides and front edge of the drawer bottoms. The bevels should slide easily into the drawers. Draw a line on the inside of the bottom where it meets the drawer back.

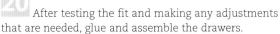

20 After testing the fit and making any adjustments that are needed, glue and assemble the drawers.

23 Place a little glue in the center of the drawer-bottom groove in the drawer front and slide the bottom in place. Drill a pilot hole into the drawer back through the saw kerf . Using a reproduction nail, install it in the pilot hole nail the drawer bottom in place. The glue holds the bottom tightly to the front while the kerf lets the bottom expand and contract. Cut the edge banding to size and, using glue and brads, install the edge banding on the edges of the drawer fronts.

22 Set the height of the table saw blade to touch the line you just drew on the drawer bottom. Use a miter gauge with an extended fence to help guide the part and cut a groove (or two equally spaced grooves for the longer drawers) in the drawer bottoms.

24 Using a straight bit in the router table, set the height to $5/8$" (16mm) and set your fence to create a $3/16$" (5mm) deep rabbit. Cut the rabbet on all four edges of the drawer fronts. Mill the drawer edge beading to size and, using a $3/16$" (5mm) corner-beading bit, roundover the front edges of the beading. Cut the edge beading (using mitered corners) to fit each drawer and attach the beading using glue and brads.

25 Sand the completed piece using 150-grit sandpaper. Then wipe down the piece with a wet rag. This will raise the grain. Once it's dry, sand it again with 180-grit sandpaper. Mix a water-based aniline dye stain to your color preference and flood the piece completely with the dye.

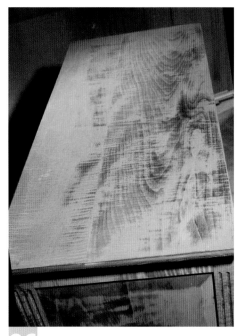

27 Liberally coat the dyed parts with boiled linseed oil. Be sure to keep it wet (applying more if needed) for 5 minutes, then wipe off the excess.

26 Let the dye sit for 5 to 10 minutes and wipe off the excess. Once that has dried, sand it lightly with 320-grit sandpaper to smooth the raised grain. This dye can look blotchy when it dries, especially on highly-figured wood. Don't panic. It's not finished yet!

28 Let the oil dry, then apply three coats of sanding sealer, sanding lightly between coats with 320-grit sandpaper. For the top coat, apply three to five coats of shellac, letting it dry completely between coats. Let the shellac cure for a week, then buff the piece with No.0000 steel wool and wax. Install the hardware. Finally, cut the backboards to size and install them using square nails, one at each end of each backboard.

two-drawer *valet*

The design and character of this project drew me to it right away. Because the night stand is built onto a chest, it's small enough to fit into any room but still large enough to store your clothes.

Add to it the 48" (122cm)-tall mirror to be sure you look your best before you walk out the door.

I'm told that the cabinet space was used for storing a hat or shoes. You could easily add small adjustable shelving to organize the space further.

by Dave Griessmann

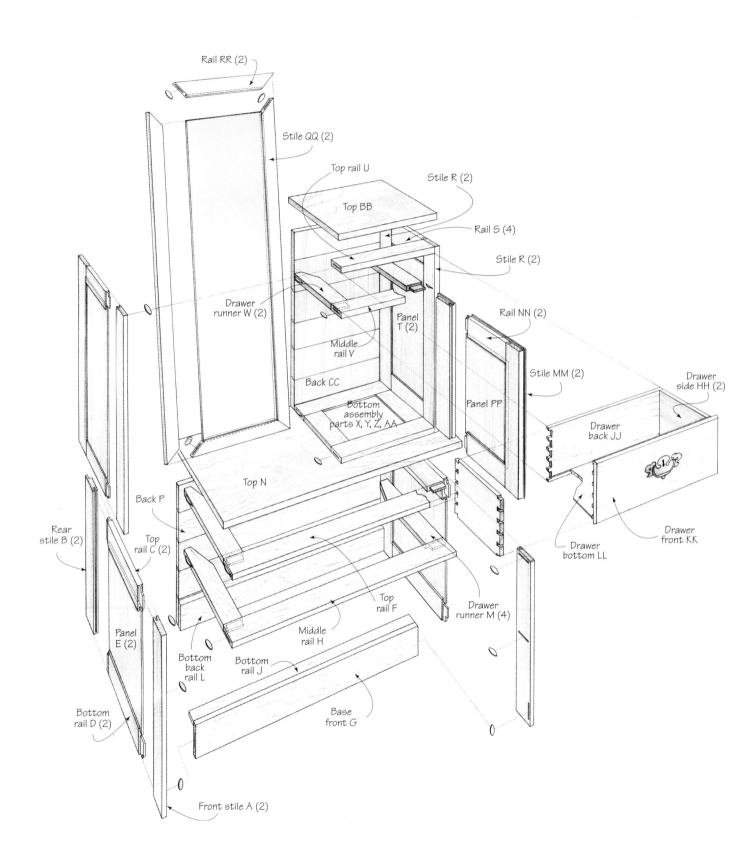

Rail RR (2)

Stile QQ (2)

Top rail U

Stile R (2)

Top BB

Rail S (4)

Stile R (2)

Drawer
runner W (2)

Rail NN (2)

Middle
rail V

Panel
T (2)

Stile MM (2)

Drawer
side HH (2)

Back CC

Panel PP

Drawer
back JJ

Bottom
assembly
parts X, Y, Z, AA

Top N

Drawer
back KK

Back P

Drawer
front KK

Rear
stile B (2)

Top
rail C (2)

Top
rail F

Drawer
runner M (4)

Drawer
bottom LL

Panel
E (2)

Middle
rail H

Bottom
back
rail L

Bottom
rail J

Bottom
rail D (2)

Base
front G

Front stile A (2)

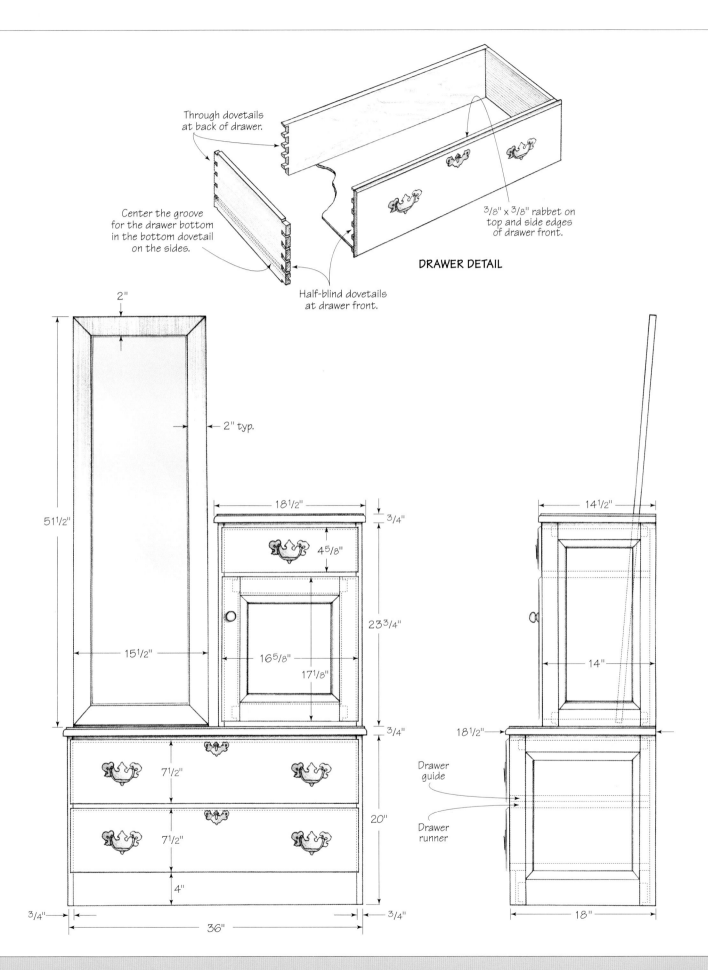

Through dovetails at back of drawer.

Center the groove for the drawer bottom in the bottom dovetail on the sides.

Half-blind dovetails at drawer front.

3/8" x 3/8" rabbet on top and side edges of drawer front.

DRAWER DETAIL

2"

2" typ.

51 1/2"

15 1/2"

18 1/2"

3/4"

4 5/8"

23 3/4"

16 5/8"

17 1/8"

3/4"

7 1/2"

7 1/2"

4"

20"

3/4"

36"

3/4"

14 1/2"

14"

18 1/2"

Drawer guide

Drawer runner

18"

CUTTING LIST ■ *two-drawer valet* inches (millimeters)

REFERENCE	QUANTITY	PART	STOCK	THICKNESS		WIDTH		LENGTH		COMMENTS
Bottom cabinet										
A	2	front stiles	cherry	¾	(19)	2	(51)	20	(508)	⅜" (10) groove
B	2	rear stiles	cherry	¾	(19)	2	(51)	20"	(508)	⅜" (10) groove and ⅜" (10) × ¾" (19) rabb
C	2	top rails	cherry	¾	(19)	2	(51)	16	(406)	1" (25) haunched tenons both ends
D	2	bottom rails	cherry	¾	(19)	4	(102)	16	(406)	1" (25) haunched tenons both ends
E	2	panels	cherry	½	(13)	14⅝	(371)	14⅝	(371)	¼" (6) × ⁵⁄₁₆" (8) rabbet all edges
F	1	top rail	cherry	¾	(19)	2	(51)	34½	(876)	
G	1	base front	cherry	¾	(19)	4	(102)	34½	(876)	
H	1	middle rail	cherry	¾	(19)	2	(51)	34½	(876)	
J	1	bottom rail	poplar	¾	(19)	1¼	(32)	34½	(876)	
K	1	top back rail	poplar	¾	(19)	2	(51)	34½	(876)	
L	1	bottom back rail	poplar	¾	(19)	4¼	(108)	34½	(876)	
M	4	drawer runners	poplar	¾	(19)	1½	(38)	15¾	(400)	¼" (6) × ½" (13) × 1" (25) tenon one end
N	1	top	cherry	¾	(19)	37	(940)	18½	(470)	
P	1	back	baltic birch	½	(13)	20	(508)	35¼	(895)	
Top cabinet										
Q	2	front stiles	cherry	¾	(19)	2	(51)	23¾	(603)	⅜" (10) groove
R	2	rear stiles	cherry	¾	(19)	2	(51)	23¾	(603)	⅜" (10) groove and ⅜" (10) × ¾" (19) rabb
S	4	rails	cherry	¾	(19)	2	(51)	12	(305)	1" (25) haunched tenon both ends
T	2	panels	cherry	½	(13)	10⅝	(270)	20⅜	(518)	¼" (6) × ⁵⁄₁₆" (8) rabbet all edges
U	1	top rail	cherry	¾	(19)	2	(51)	16	(406)	
V	1	middle rail	cherry	¾	(19)	2	(51)	16	(406)	
W	2	drawer runners	poplar	¾	(19)	1½	(38)	11¾	(298)	¼" (6) × ½" (13) × 1" (25) tenon one end
X	1	front bottom stile*	cherry	¾	(19)	2	(51)	16	(406)	* parts X, Y, Z and AA make up the top cabinet's bottom
Y	1	back bottom stile*	poplar	¾	(19)	2	(51)	16	(406)	
Z	2	bottom rails*	poplar	¾	(19)	2	(51)	11¼	(286)	1" (25) tenons both ends
AA	1	bottom panel*	poplar	¾	(19)	12¼	(311)	9½	(241)	¼" (6) × ¼" (6) tongue all edges
BB	1	top	cherry	¾	(19)	18½	(470)	14½	(368)	
CC	1	back	baltic birch	½	(13)	12¾	(324)	23¾	(603)	
Lower drawers										
DD	4	drawer sides	poplar	½	(13)	7⅛	(181)	16	(406)	
EE	2	drawer backs	poplar	½	(13)	6⅜	(162)	34⅜	(873)	
FF	2	drawer fronts	cherry	¾	(19)	7½	(191)	35⅛	(892)	rabbet top and sides
GG	2	drawer bottoms	poplar	⅝	(16)	33⅜	(848)	16¼	(413)	
Upper drawer										
HH	2	drawer sides	poplar	½	(13)	4⅞	(124)	12	(305)	
JJ	1	drawer back	poplar	½	(13)	4⅛	(105)	16	(406)	
KK	1	drawer front	cherry	¾	(19)	5¼	(133)	16⅝	(422)	rabbet top and sides
LL	1	drawer bottom	plywood	¼	(6)	15	(381)	16	(406)	
Upper door										
MM	2	stiles	cherry	¾	(19)	2	(51)	17⅛	(435)	⅜" (10) groove
NN	2	rails	cherry	¾	(19)	2	(51)	14½	(368)	⅜" (10) groove, ⅜" (10) × ½" (13) haunched tenon both ends
PP	1	panel	cherry	½	(13)	13⅛	(333)	13⅝	(346)	⅜" (10) × ⅝" (16) rabbet 3 sides, ⅜" (10) × ⅛" (3) rabbet 1 side
Mirror frame (This frame will fit a 12 (305) × 48 (1219) mirror.)										
QQ	2	stiles	cherry	¾	(19)	2	(51)	51½	(1307)	both ends mitered and slotted for biscu
RR	2	rails	cherry	¾	(19)	2	(51)	15½	(394)	both ends mitered and slotted for biscu
SS	1	back	plywood	⅛	(3)	12½	(318)	48½	(1232)	

hardware & supplies

- 5—drawer pulls
- 2—escutcheon plates
- 1—door knob
- 2—butt hinges

2 Set up a ¹/₄" (6mm) mortising bit in a mortising machine to cut 1" (25mm) deep. Mark your mortise positions and cut the mortises.

1 Cut all stiles and rails according to the cutting list. Set the height of the table saw blade to ³/₈" (9mm) and the fence ¹/₄" (6mm) away from the blade. Cut a groove in the rails and stiles in the side panels for both the top and bottom cabinets. Then turn the parts end for end and make another cut. This will create a ³/₈"-deep × ¹/₄"-wide (9mm × 6mm) groove in the center of each piece.

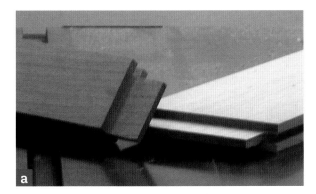

a

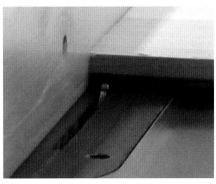

4 Cut out the top and bottom cabinet side panels and make a ³/₈" × ¹/₄" (9mm × 6mm) rabbet on all four sides of each panel. This will create a ³/₈"-wide × ¹/₄"-long (9mm × 6mm) tongue on the panels.

b

3 Make the tenons by clamping a ¹/₄"-thick (6mm) set-off block to the fence. Then set the blade height to ¹/₄" (6mm) and the fence at 1¹/₄" (32mm). With the rail flat on the saw, use a miter gauge to guide the parts and make the shoulder cuts on both sides of the rails. Make repeat cuts, moving away from the fence, wasting away material a kerf at a time until leaving the ¹/₄" (6mm) tenon. Set the fence on the band saw ³/₈" (9mm) from the blade and cut the haunches on the tenons. Finally, cut a ⁷/₁₆" × ³/₄" (11mm × 19mm) rabbet on the back two stiles of your upper and lower cases. They will receive the cabinet backs.

5 Test the fit of the panels in the grooves and adjust as needed. Once you have a snug fit, glue up the sides.

6 Make the bottom assembly for the top cabinet.

7 Cut ¼" × ½" × 1" (6mm × 13mm × 25mm) mortises in the back edges of the drawer dividers and top and bottom drawer rails. Also, mark and cut a slot for a No.0 biscuit in the case sides and the ends of the rails and drawer dividers.

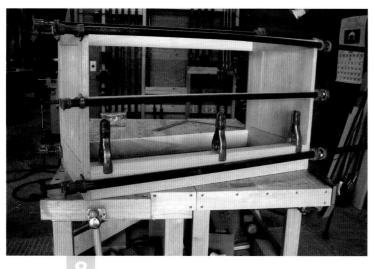

8 Dry assemble the cabinets to check for the proper fit of all parts. If all is OK, glue up both cabinet assemblies.

9 Cut some ¾" × ¾" (19mm × 19mm) cleat material to length as shown in the photo. Using glue and brads, attach the cleats to the top side rails and the back rail. Then glue the lower rail to the inside top of the base.

10 Cut out the tops for both cases and use a ⅜" (9mm) roundover bit to shape the edges on the underside of the tops. Then use a ³⁄₁₆" (5mm) roundover bit set to cut a ¼" (6mm) ledge and round over the top's sides. This will add decorative look.

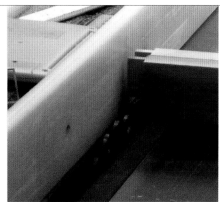

12 Cut ¼"-thick × ½"-wide × 1"-long (6mm × 13mm × 25mm) tenons on one end of the drawer runners and kickers, and drill a screw hole in the other ends.

11 Drill oversize holes (to allow seasonal movement) through the cleats and the top front rail on the bottom cabinet and the top rails on the top cabinet. Then lay the tops upside down on the bench and attach them to the cases using 1¼"-(30mm) long screws.

13 Line up a carpenter's square on the drawer divider and along the case, and mark the locations of the drawer runners on the case sides.

14 Add glue to the tenons on the runners and insert the tenon in the mortise in the back of the drawer divider. Hold the runner flush with the line and install a screw to hold the runner in place. The angle cut on the back of the runner is purely cosmetic.

15 To determine the drawer front sizes, measure the drawer openings and add ⅝" (16mm) to the length and ¼" (6mm) to the width. Use a 3/16" (5mm) roundover bit set to cut a ¼"(6mm) ledge and rout all four edges of each drawer front.

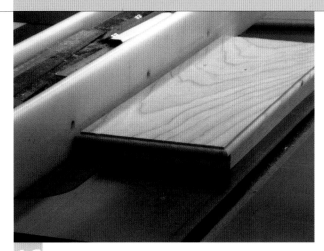

16 Set the table saw blade at $^5/_{16}$" (8mm) and the fence $^5/_{16}$" (8mm) from the blade. Make a cut on the top edge and both end edges with the drawer face against the fence. Lay a drawer front face up on the table saw and set the blade height so it's even with the top of the cut you just made. Set the fence $^1/_4$" (6mm) from the blade. (This setup is assuming a $^1/_8$" (3mm) blade thickness.) With the drawer fronts facing up, make the second cut to create the rabbets.

17 Test the fit of the drawer fronts. The inside length (from rabbet to rabbet) should be about $^1/_8$" (3mm) less than the drawer openings.

18 Cut the door parts to size. The door uses the same mortise-and-tenon joinery as the side-panel assemblies of the cabinet. Rout the same profile that is used on the drawer fronts.

19 With the door facing out and the hinge side up, secure the door in a vise or clamps. Mark the locations for the door hinges and, using a chisel, cut the edges of the mortise.

20 Using a router set up with a straight-cutting bit, set the bit to cut the same depth as the mortise. Rout out the bulk of the material and clean up with a chisel.

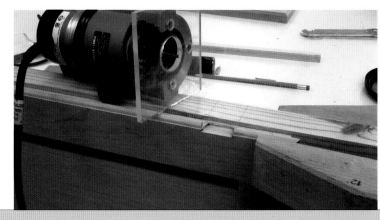

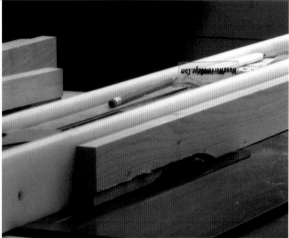

21 Cut rabbets on the top, bottom and left side of the door as was done on the drawer fronts. Cut a ⅛"-wide (3mm) rabbet on the hinge side. You may have to adjust the hinge-side mortise so the door will close. Then, using chisels and router, cut the matching hinge mortise in the top cabinet's side.

22 Cut out the mirror frame parts. Set the saw blade height to ½" (13mm) and the fence ⅝" (16mm) away from the blade. Make the cut on the inside edges of the parts. If the mirror is ⅛"-thick (3mm), move on to step 23. If the mirror is ¼"-thick (6mm), move the fence ⅛" (3mm) closer to the blade and make another cut.

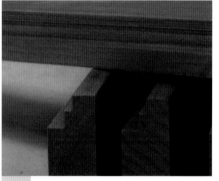

23 Set the blade height to ¼" (6mm) high and move the fence ⅛" (3mm) closer to the blade and make the cut. This creates a double rabbet—one to hold the mirror and the other to hold the back.

24 Buy the mirror before cutting its frame parts to length. Then you can cut the parts to fit the mirror. Cut No.0 biscuit slots in the face of the miter cuts and assemble the frame. Rout the same profile on the mirror frame that you used on the door and drawer fronts.

25 Cut the backs to size and install them using brads or screws.

26 Sand all parts and apply the stain (if desired) and top coats. Install the mirror in its frame and the ⅛" (3mm) plywood back. Use brads to hold the back in place. Finally, install the hardware and apply a coat of wax.

drop-front *secretary*

The drop-front is a traditional piece of furniture found in most farm houses and homes built in the early 20th century and is ideally located in a living room, bedroom, den or office. However, I remember seeing a tired-looking drop-front desk in an equally tired-looking barn. I felt bad for them both.

Variations in design can include locks on the doors, drawers instead of a door in the lower section below the drop desktop and a plywood back with veneer taped edges.

by Jim Stack

drop-front secretary inches (millimeters)

REFERENCE	QUANTITY	PART	STOCK	THICKNESS		WIDTH		LENGTH		COMMENTS
A	1	left side	cherry	¾	(19)	12	(305)	52¾	(1320)	⅜" (10mm) tenon both ends (tbe)
B	1	center partition	cherry	¾	(19)	11¼	(246)	52¾	(1320)	⅜" (10mm) tbe, mortise right side
C	1	right side	cherry	¾	(19)	12	(305)	35¾	(908)	⅜" (10mm) tbe, tapered to top
D	1	bottom	cherry	¾	(19)	13½	(343)	40¼	(1022)	three dadoes
E	1	left top	cherry	¾	(19)	12¾	(337)	20¾	(527)	two dadoes
F	1	right top	cherry	¾	(19)	9	(229)	20	(508)	one dado, ⅜" (10mm) tenon one end
G	1	desk shelf	cherry	¾	(19)	10½	(267)	19¼	(489)	⅜" (10mm) tbe
H	1	front rail	cherry	¾	(19)	3½	(89)	20⅜	(518)	both ends notched. miter right end
I	1	attached moulding*	cherry	⅜	(10)	¾	(19)	13*	(330)	miter one end, *cut length to fit
J	2	base front and back	cherry	¾	(19)	4	(102)	39½	(997)	mitered both ends
K	2	base ends	cherry	¾	(19)	4	(102)	12	(305)	mitered both ends
L	4	feet	cherry	3	(76)	3	(76)	8¾	(222)	
M	2	corner blocks	cherry	¾	(19)	3	(76)	3	(76)	
N	2	cleats	cherry	¾	(19)	¾	(19)	32	(813)	
P	2	cleats	cherry	¾	(19)	¾	(19)	7	(178)	
Q	4	shelves*	cherry	¾	(19)	11	(279)	18⁷⁄₁₆	(468)	*or ¼ (6mm) tempered glass shelves

Back

REFERENCE	QUANTITY	PART	STOCK	THICKNESS		WIDTH		LENGTH		COMMENTS
R	2	stiles	cherry	¾	(19)	3	(76)	58	(1473)	cut to length after back is assembled
S	1	center stile	cherry	¾	(19)	3	(76)	48	(1219)	¾" (19mm) tbe
T	1	crest rail	cherry	¾	(19)	12	(76)	34½	(876)	¾" (19mm) tbe
U	1	bottom rail	cherry	¾	(19)	3	(76)	34½	(876)	¾" (19mm) tbe
V	2	panels	cherry	½	(13)	15⅝	(397)	47	(1194)	

Cubby Assembly

REFERENCE	QUANTITY	PART	STOCK	THICKNESS		WIDTH		LENGTH		COMMENTS
W	2	top and bottom	cherry	¼	(6)	6	(152)	18⁷⁄₁₆	(468)	
X	7	dividers	cherry	¼	(6)	6	(152)	5¾	(146)	grain runs vertically
Y	2	cleats	cherry	¼	(6)	2	(51)	6	(152)	
Z	2	pencil holders	cherry	¾	(19)	1	(25)	6	(152)	

Doors

REFERENCE	QUANTITY	PART	STOCK	THICKNESS		WIDTH		LENGTH		COMMENTS
AA	2	drop-top stiles	cherry	¾	(19)	2¼	(57)	13⅞	(352)	¾" (19mm) tbe
BB	2	drop-top rails	cherry	¾	(19)	2¼	(57)	18⅜	(467)	
CC	2	drop-top panel	cherry	¾	(19)	13⅝	(346)	15⅜	(391)	
DD	2	bottom-door stiles	cherry	¾	(19)	2¼	(57)	18⅛	(460)	
EE	2	bottom-door rails	cherry	¾	(19)	2¼	(57)	15⅜	(391)	¾" (19mm) tbe
FF	1	bottom-door panel	cherry	½	(13)	15⅛	(384)	15⅛	(384)	
GG	2	tall-door stiles	cherry	¾	(19)	2¼	(57)	51¾	(1314)	
HH	2	tall-door rails	cherry	¾	(19)	2¼	(57)	15⅜	(391)	¾" (19mm) tbe

Mirror Frame

REFERENCE	QUANTITY	PART	STOCK	THICKNESS		WIDTH		LENGTH		COMMENTS
JJ	2	stiles	cherry	¾	(19)	2	(51)	16	(406)	
KK	1	rail	cherry	¾	(19)	2	(51)	19	(483)	
LL	1	crest rail	cherry	¾	(19)	4¼	(108)	16	(406)	

hardware & supplies

- 5—2½" (65mm) × 1½" (40mm) brass ball end hinges
- 3—door handles
- 2—brass stays
- 2—brass butler-tray hinges
- 3—magnetic catches
- 16—5mm shelf pins

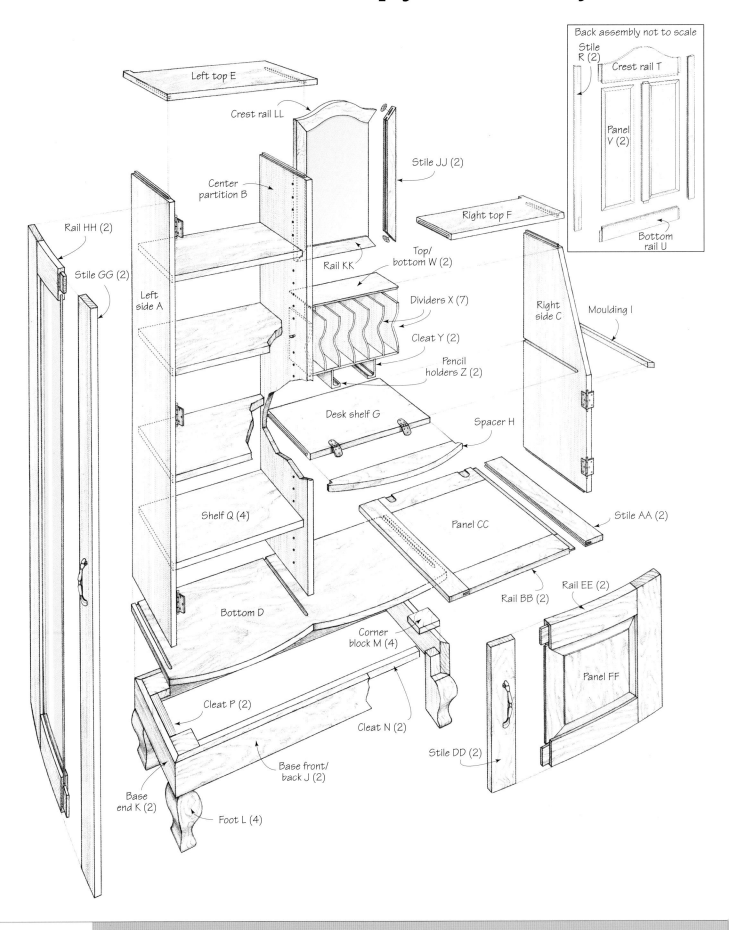

Back assembly not to scale

Stile R (2)

Crest rail T

Panel V (2)

Bottom rail U

Left top E

Crest rail LL

Stile JJ (2)

Center partition B

Right top F

Rail HH (2)

Rail KK

Top/ bottom W (2)

Stile GG (2)

Dividers X (7)

Right side C

Moulding I

Left side A

Cleat Y (2)

Pencil holders Z (2)

Desk shelf G

Spacer H

Shelf Q (4)

Stile AA (2)

Panel CC

Rail EE (2)

Rail BB (2)

Bottom D

Corner block M (4)

Panel FF

Cleat P (2)

Cleat N (2)

Stile DD (2)

Base front/ back J (2)

Base end K (2)

Foot L (4)

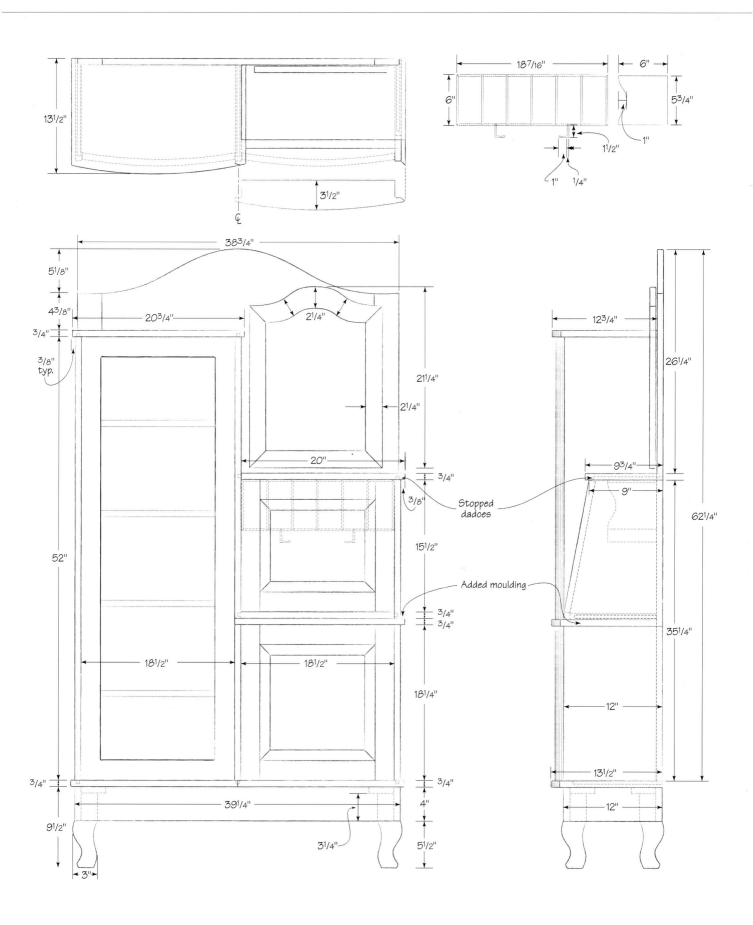

13 1/2"

3 1/2"

18 7/16"   6"

6"   5 3/4"

1 1/2"   1"

1"   1/4"

38 3/4"

5 1/8"

4 3/8"

3/4"

3/8" typ.

20 3/4"

2 1/4"

2 1/4"

21 1/4"

20"

3/4"

3/8"

Stopped dadoes

15 1/2"

52"

Added moulding

18 1/2"

18 1/2"

18 1/4"

3/4"
3/4"

3/4"

9 1/2"

3"

39 1/4"

3 1/4"

4"

5 1/2"

3/4"

12 3/4"

26 1/4"

9 3/4"

9"

62 1/4"

35 1/4"

12"

13 1/2"

12"

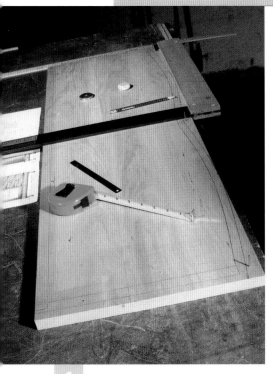

1 I cut the bottom to size and drew the full-scale plans on it. Include as many details as possible—where the partitions, sides, doors and back are located and what type of joinery will be used. As I was building the cabinet, I used this drawing as my template for all the other parts. There's nothing as frustrating as miscut parts, dadoes or tenons located in the wrong place. A clear layout will save time, material, lots of yelling, sanity and a big headache. Yeah, it's that important to make these drawings correct.

2 After the drawing is made and you understand how the project is to be assembled, cut out the aprons for the base. Miter the corners, apply glue to the miters and use band clamps to hold the assembly together while the glue dries. Never fear, the glued butt joints will be ok. As shown later, the legs and the corner blocks will make this base strong enough to support dancing elephants.

3 While the base apron assembly is drying, make a pattern for the feet. I used $\frac{1}{8}$" (3mm) hardboard, but stiff cardboard will also work. The pattern doesn't need to be perfect, it just needs to be a pleasing shape with smooth lines. You're going to use this to trace the profile on the foot blanks.

4 Mill the foot blanks square and cut them to length. Set the table saw's fence to $3\frac{1}{4}$" (83mm)(including the width of the saw blade) and the blade height to $\frac{3}{4}$" (19mm). Make a cut, as shown in the photo on two adjacent sides of each foot blank. You're on your way to creating tenons on the feet.

5 Set the band saw's fence to $2\frac{1}{4}$" (57mm) and make the two long tenon cuts, stopping at the table saw cut, to create a tenon on each foot. If you don't trust yourself to stop cutting at the table saw cut, use wood scrap as a stop block. (It's obvious I don't trust myself.)

6 Now for some fun. Get the pattern you made in Step 3, grab a pencil and trace the foot profile on the outside of each foot. Make the cut as shown. Then trace the profile on the side with the cut you just made. Now make this second cut.

7 Reverse the pattern and trace the profile on the inside of the feet. Make that cut, then trace the profile on this cut and make the final profile cut as shown above. The cuts are safe to make because the feet are supported at two points on the band saw table.

8 Sand the feet until they're smooth with a nice flow to the lines of the profile. An ocillating spindle sander is the tool of choice for this type of sanding but a cut off broom handle with sandpaper wrapped around it will also work. Trust me, it's been done before.

9 Cut the corner blocks and glue them in place. Then flip the apron assembly over, put glue on the top and both sides of each foot tenon and glue the feet into place. Clamp from both sides of each foot. Clamping downward is optional but I wanted to be sure each foot was firmly held in place.

10 Double, no, triple check the cutting list, then cut out the sides, shelves and tops. (If you're using plywood, this is easy. If you're using hardwood, you may need to glue parts to width.) Also, if you're using biscuit joinery, ignore this stuff about cutting mortises and tenons. Ok, here's the stuff about cutting the mortises. Carefully layout the mortises (measure thrice, cut once), make a jig [¹⁄₂" (12mm) or ³⁄₄" (18mm) MDF] like the one in the photo. It guides the router while ploughing the mortise.

11 The tenons on the parts can be cut using the table saw or a router table. I used a rabbeting bit for making these cuts. Cut one side of the part, flip it over and cut the other side. Use some scrap wood the same thickness as your parts to setup the cuts so the tenon is the correct width. Trim the tenons at the front edges of the parts where they meet the stopped mortises. Triple check everything for fit, then assemble the cabinet. Refer to the illustrations as often as needed so you don't mess up.

12 After cutting the grooves in the back and drop-front panel parts, I mark the center location of the table saw blade (Photo a). (When the blade is raised, this is the highest point of the blade above the table.) Then I raise the blade to the required depth of the mortises. Half of the mortises are cut straight into the parts (Photo c), half are plunge cuts (Photo c and d). Stop the cuts when the blade centerline mark and the rail location marks line up. The back of the saw blade will cut past the mortise locations but it's OK. The panels will cover these slightly deeper cuts.

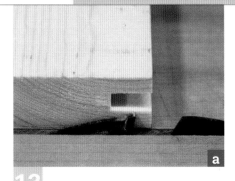

13 To cut the tenons on the rails, set the table saw's fence (including the blade thickness) to the length of the tenon and set the blade height to about one-third of the thickness of the rails (Photo a). Use test pieces to fine-tune the setup. Then nibble away the material to create the tenons (Photos b and c). Panels will cover these slightly deeper cuts.

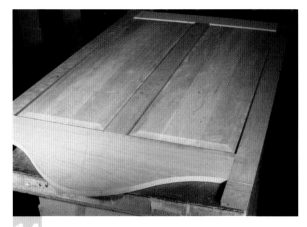

14 To assemble the back, apply glue only at the stile-and-rail joints. Then put the center stile in place on each rail, slide the panels in place and attache the outside stiles. Put a clamp across each rail and one from top to bottom to pull the joints together.

15 I drew a square line on both of the back's outside stiles where they meet the crest rail. This line guided me as I blended the crest rail curve into the tops of the stiles. When all the cabinet parts have been cut and dry-fitted, it's time to assemble the cabinet. Use the illustrations to help you put things together properly.

16 I prefer laminated bending over steam bending because the results can be predicted. The springback of laminated parts is zero, whereas steam-bent parts tend to straighten a little when they're taken from the mold and that springback can't be determined with much accuracy. The radius of the bend will determine the thickness of the laminations, which will result in zero springback if the laminations are the correct thickness. For this project, 1/8" (3mm)-thick laminations were perfect. Determine the radius for the door rails by referencing your full-scale drawing. Make a gluing jig to this radius, wax the curved surface of the jig so the glue won't stick to it and make the door rails. Let each rail sit 24 hours in the jig

17 Use the scrap from making the rail-gluing jig as a guide for routing the groove in the center of the curved door rails. Make a shallow pass, then raise the bit and make another pass. Do this until you reach the proper groove depth. Use this same router bit to cut the grooves in the door stiles.

18 I used the router table to cut the grooves in the curved-doors' parts. After cutting the grooves in the parts, raise the bit to the depth of the mortises. On the router table fence, mark both sides of the router bit (Photos a and b). Use the right hand mark as the stopping point for the straight-in cuts (Photo c) and the left hand mark for the start of the plunge cuts (Photo d).

19 Cut the curved rails to length. Reference your full-scale drawing to determine the angle of the cut. At the ends of each rail, the cut should be 90 degrees to the curve. Of course, this isn't really true, but visualize about 1" (25mm) of the ends of the rails and pretend that that part is straight and gauge your cut from it.

20 Use a tenoning fixture with a wedge attached to it to hold the rails so their cut ends rest flat on the top of the table saw. Set up the fixture and cut the tenons so they fit snugly into the grooves in the stiles. Assemble the glass door frame. Then use a rabbeting bit to cut the rabbets for the glass. The router will sit flat enough on the curved rails. You'll need to square the corners of the rabbets with a chisel. See suppliers list for ordering curved glass.

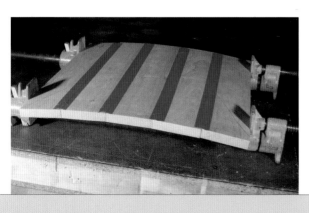

21 I used 5 boards to make the curved door panel. Using more boards means less work to create the curve. The outside of the panel has a 54" (137cm) radius. The panel uses 16.2° of the circumference of the circle. Divide that by 5. The angle of each edge-to-edge joint is 3.25°. Divide that by 2. The miter cut is 1.62°—give or take a little. Make slight adjustments as needed to make the required radius. When the door panel dry-fits to the correct curve, lay the parts face up, tape the joints, turn the assembly over, apply glue in the bevel joints and fold them together. Use gentle clamping pressure to hold the panel until the glue cures (24 hours).

22 To start creating the curve on the panel, break out your handplane and level the joints until they start blending with the flat surfaces of the boards.

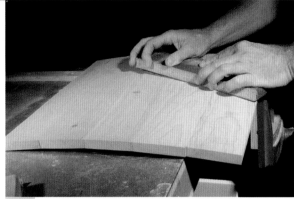

23 This is the best way to true the curve: use an 80-grit sanding belt wrapped around a wood block and sand across the wood grain. Then use a random orbital sander to clean it up.

24 Use a curved scraper to roughout the curve on the inside of the panel. Finish up with the random orbital sander.

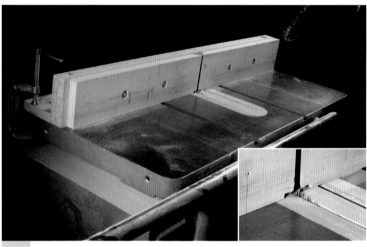

25 My good friend, the late Danny Proulx, showed me this method of cutting raised panels using the table saw. Set up a fence centered on (front to back) and at a right angle to the blade (I used the fence from my router table). Use a carbide-tipped saw blade and raise it 1/8" (3mm). Do not try to cut any deeper at anytime.

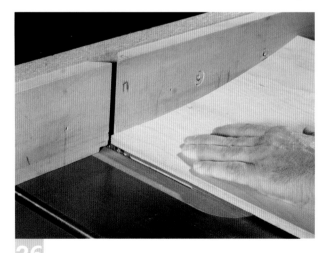

26 The great part about using this panel-making method is that it works for making the curved raised panel.

27 The slower you feed the panel past the saw blade, the smoother the cut. Cleanup the cuts using a scraper and sandpaper.

28 Lay out the shape of the mirror-frame top rail and cut it.

29 Sand the curves of the rail smooth. Then use a rabbeting bit to cut rabbets in the mirror frame's parts.

30 Cut the miters on the mirror frame parts, cut a slot in the miters for a No.1 biscuit and assemble the frame using a band clamp. Check the frame for squareness and let the glue dry. Make a template for the mirror, take it to your local hardware store and have them cut you a mirror. The hardware store folks like it when I come in with something out of the ordinary and I like the personal attention (which I usually don't get at a large chain homebuilding center).

31 I've been installing butt hinges for years using jigs just like this one. They're easy to make and do the job quickly and accurately. Cut the mortise $1/16$" (2mm) less that the thickness of the closed hinge. When the hinge is installed, this will automatically create the spacing between the hinge side of the door and the cabinet. See photo 32. Square the corners of the mortise.

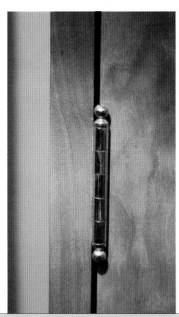

32 Install the butt hinges on the door. Then draw a line where the screws of the hinges will be located on the inside of the cabinet. Rest the door on a spacer on the bottom of the cabinet and drill one pilot hole at the top hinge. Install the screw and gently close the door to check its alignment to the face of the cabinet. Note any door in-or-out adjustments that need to be made. Open the door and install a screw in the bottom hinge, accounting for the adjustment if necessary. Repeat the closing and checking of the door's alignment. When all is to your liking, install the remaining screws.

33 I made a jig for cutting the mortises for the drop-leaf desktop. Note the blue tape used to fine tune the fit of the mortise to the hinge plate exactly.

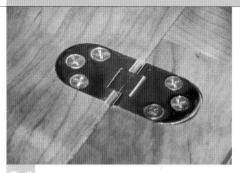

34 When the desk is opened, your eye is immediately drawn to the bright brass hinges, so make them a good fit. The drop-front desktop and the shelf it's hinged to need to be flush when the desktop is open. The butler tray hinges look good and work perfectly. The installation of the hinges is just like the butt hinge installation. Install the hinges on the desktop first, then attach them to the shelf.

35 After the cabinet is completely assembled, add this filler on the tops. It "wraps" the top around the back and closes the gap between the two. You could attach these fillers before you install the tops but it's a fragile assembly at best.

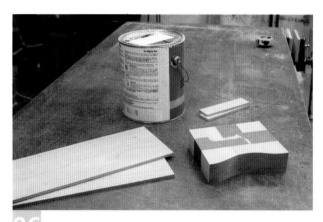

36 Cut the parts for the cubby holes. Stack and tape the vertical dividers together. Draw a curve on the front edges (I used the bottom of the paint can in the photo as my template) and cut the whole mess in one shot on the band saw. Then sand them, blending the curve with a slight radius to make a pleasing shape.

37 I cut the dadoes for the vertical cubby hole dividers using a router table. The table saw will work equally as well.

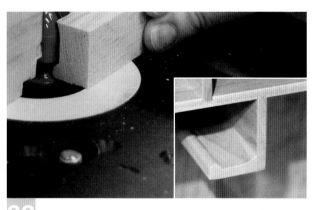

38 I used a mutiprofile router bit to make the pencil holders. Make one long piece, glue the bracket to it and cut the lengths required. The cubby assembly is nailed together. Predrill for the nails so the vertical dividers don't split.

39 After finish-sanding the entire project, I used a paintbrush to apply ammonia to the raw wood. (The left side of the wood sample in the photo shows how the ammonia affects the cherry.) After the ammonia dried, I sanded the raised grain and applied a coat of catalyzed lacquer. When the lacquer was dry, I sanded the finish using 220-grit sandpaper. I applied two additional coats of lacquer and allowed them to cure for one week, then used No.0000 steel wool to rub the finish. To make the finish a little shinier, I applied a coat of wax.

suppliers

**Adams & Kennedy—
The Wood Source**
6178 Mitch Owen Rd.
P.O. Box 700
Manotick, ON
Canada K4M 1A6
613-822-6800
www.wood-source.com
Wood supply

Adjustable Clamp Company
404 N. Armour St.
Chicago, IL 60622
312-666-0640
www.adjustableclamp.com
Clamps and woodworking tools

B&Q
Portswood House
1 Hampshire Corporate Park
Chandlers Ford
Eastleigh
Hampshire, England SO53 3YX
0845 609 6688
www.diy.com
*Woodworking tools, supplies
and hardware*

Busy Bee Tools
130 Great Gulf Dr.
Concord, ON
Canada L4K 5W1
1-800-461-2879
www.busybeetools.com
Woodworking tools and supplies

**Constantine's Wood
Center of Florida**
1040 E. Oakland Park Blvd.
Fort Lauderdale, FL 33334
800-443-9667
www.constantines.com
Tools, woods, veneers, hardware

**Frank Paxton
Lumber Company**
5701 W. Sixty-sixth St.
Chicago, IL 60638
800-323-2203
www.paxtonwood.com
Wood, hardware, tools, books

The Home Depot
2455 Paces Ferry Rd.
Atlanta, GA 30339
800-553-3199 (U.S.)
800-628-0525 (Canada)
www.homedepot.com
*Woodworking tools, supplies
and hardware*

Lee Valley Tools Ltd.
P.O. Box 1780
Ogdensburg, NY 13669-6780
800-871-8158 (U.S.)
800-267-8767 (Canada)
www.leevalley.com
Woodworking tools and hardware

Klingspor Abrasives Inc.
2555 Tate Blvd. SE
Hickory, NC 28602
800-645-5555
www.klingspor.com
Sandpaper of all kinds

Lowe's
P.O. Box 1111
North Wilkesboro, NC 28656
800-445-6937
www.lowes.com
Woodworking tools, supplies and hardware

**Rockler Woodworking
and Hardware**
4365 Willow Dr.
Medina, MN 55340
800-279-4441
www.rockler.com
Woodworking tools, hardware and books

Tool Trend Ltd.
140 Snow Blvd.
Thornhill, ON
Canada L4K 4L1
416-663-8665
Woodworking tools and hardware

**Trend Machinery and
Cutting Tools Ltd.**
Odhams Trading Estate
St. Albans Rd.
Watford
Hertfordshire, U.K.
WD24 7TR
01923 224657
www.trendmachinery.co.uk
Woodworking tools and hardware

**Vaughan & Bushnell
Manufacturing Co.**
11414 Maple Ave.
Hebron, IL 60034
815-648-2446
www.vaughanmfg.com
Hammers and other tools

Waterlox
800-321-0377
www.waterlox.com
Finishing supplies

Woodcraft Supply Corp.
1177 Rosemar Rd.
P.O. Box 1686
Parkersburg, WV 26102
800-535-4482
www.woodcraft.com
Woodworking hardware

Woodworker's Hardware
P.O. Box 180
Sauk Rapids, MN 56379-0180
800-383-0130
www.wwhardware.com
*Woodworking hardware, bed rail
connectors*

Woodworker's Supply
1108 N. Glenn Rd.
Casper, WY 82601
800-645-9292
http://woodworker.com
*Woodworking tools and accessories,
finishing supplies, books and plans*

index